LANDMARK COLLECTOR'S LIBRARY

THE SPIRIT OF
STARBECK

Stephen G Abbott

Above: See page 127
Opposite page: See page 51

THE SPIRIT OF
STARBECK

Stephen G Abbott

Landmark Publishing

Published by

Ashbourne Hall, Cokayne Ave
Ashbourne, Derbyshire DE6 1EJ England
Tel: (01335) 347349 Fax: (01335) 347303
e-mail: landmark@clara.net
web site: www.landmarkpublishing.co.uk

1st edition

ISBN 1 84306 079 5

Printed by Bath Press Ltd, Bath.

Design & reproduction by Mark Titterton & Simon Hartshorne

Cover captions:

Front cover: A parade during the St Andrews festival of 1906
Back cover top: Robert Johnson's greengrocery and confectionary shop
Back cover middle: Starbeck Mission Sunday School trip
Back cover bottom: A Clarkson open topped double decker steam bus

www.starbeck-history.co.uk
Books, Information, Museum.

Contents

Acknowledgements

It would have been impossible to produce this book without the assistance of the following people to whom I am greatly indebted.

The majority of these pictures have come via two main sources. Firstly I must thank all my friends and colleagues at, and the visitors to, the Starbeck Museum. Here I found the majority of these photographs, the collection being mainly the work of the late Gordon Beer. I have tried my best to trace all sources of origin, but many Starbeck residents and visitors donated these pictures anonymously and remain unknown. If I could name them all I would. However, regrettably, that is impossible. A special mention should go to the kind lady who donated the Walter Smith collection. The pictures from the museum of unknown origin are here credited to the museum. Please forgive my lack of knowledge, and please accept my apology in the understanding that these pictures have been put to a good use, one for which they were intended.

I must also thank Rita Sobot, Graham Chalmers and the staff at the Harrogate Advertiser for their help and assistance and for giving me open access to the Advertiser and Herald archive. It must be added that I have always found the Harrogate Advertiser more than helpful.

May I also thank Emma Evans at Bettys' bakery for her enthusiastic assistance and the benefit of her knowledge of the company. Thanks are also due to: Councillor Pat Marsh; Wilf Blakey; Mrs Moyra Osborne; and Mr Alan Barker and his staff at Norbar for their pictures and assistance and likewise Mick Gray of the Railway Athletic FC. May I also thank Mr J Coleman the secretary of Starbeck Working Men's Club for his help and access to the club's archive pictures; Sally Bethel at Clarendon Racing who kindly supplied the information and picture of "Starbeck" the racehorse; and gratitude is also due to Paul Wood of the Harrogate & District Athletics League and their web site www.harrogate-league.co.uk. May I also thank my friends Jim and Herbert Rogers for their interest and help, not forgetting M Ellison at NERA for his guidance. Thanks also to Mr G Pierson for permission to publish his picture of the north yard. I must not overlook the contribution of Jen Little of the Empics sports photograph agency, or anybody else involved in the acquiring, collecting, identifying and developing of the many pictures in this book.

I would like to express my gratitude to Loraine of the Ken Hoole Study Centre at Darlington railway museum, and David Williamson of the North Eastern Railway Association for their invaluable help and guidance in the location of many of the railway pictures and copyright holders. The same must be said of Alan Thompson of the J W Armstrong Trust.

If I have forgotten anybody forgive me, I thanked you at the time and I thank you now.

Introduction

Tucked into it's own valley half way between the ancient castle town of Knaresborough and the rather bourgeois one time spa town of Harrogate lies Starbeck, a place with a character, atmosphere and spirit quite separate from its more illustrious neighbours. Starbeck has neither the mediaeval heritage of Knaresborough nor the Victorian grandeur of Harrogate, because this is a different place, quite separate and unaffected by both. To come here looking for the tearooms and Victoriana of Harrogate or the mediaeval charm of Knaresborough would only lead to disappointment, because those are not reflected here. The people who come here, come here to work and live in a community with a beating heart all of its own.

Starbeck's history is short, of that there is no doubt. Up to just 250 years ago there was nothing here barring a scattering of cottages and farmhouses around an unassuming mineral well. This particular part of the Royal Forest of Knaresborough was surrounded on three sides by the ancient manor of the Plompton family, the royal hunting park of Bilton, and the once monastic lands of Belmont. This then was forestland, common grazing and arable land, for use by anyone who could pay the tithe. The earliest of the scattered houses began to appear around Forest Lane Head in the 1700s, but it was well after the eventual enclosure of the forest in 1778 that Starbeck started to grow into what we know today.

Springs of mineral water had been discovered perhaps as early as the late 16th century, but the spa industry of Starbeck was never anything if not stunted; never quite gaining the fame it should have had, and never quite breaking out of the shadow of the more famous High and Low Harrogate waters.

It was the arrival of the railways in 1849 that sparked the fuse of growth here. As men came from all around the country to work the trains and goods yards the population grew at a relentless rate. Other industries were attracted by Starbeck's countrywide rail connections, to the extent that when the railways fell into an equally rapid decline in the late 1950s and 1960s, Starbeck survived without it.

There is little, if any, evidence today of the once important railway centre. Likewise the malt works, the steam corn mill, the water bottling plant, Octavius Atkinson's structural steel works, and many others are gone. Through all this Starbeck lives on, and what's more lives on with its spirit and identity intact.

It is a remarkable place, with remarkable people, a working place with working people.

Don't forget to visit www.starbeck-history.co.uk

Bettys of Harrogate

The local legend says that Frederick Belmont, Swiss Confectioner and one time orphan, came to England in 1907 with little more than a vision of quality and the skill to fulfil his ambitions. The legend also states that when he arrived in Yorkshire it was only because he had boarded the wrong train. However, when finally he reached Harrogate in 1910 he found the bracing air reminiscent of his homeland and decided to stay. After marrying his landlady's daughter Clare in 1917, Clare's widowed aunt, Mary, helped set them up with their own business, a continental style café originally in Cambridge Crescent almost opposite today's more familiar establishment.

They began their long association with Starbeck in 1922, when they opened their bakery on Prospect Road. Since then, as a credit to themselves and all that Frederick Belmont envisaged, Bettys of Harrogate has continued to produce the finest quality products, here in Starbeck. In 1962 Frederick Belmont's nephew and heir bought out the business of Taylors' tea and coffee. Soon Taylors' Café Imperials in Harrogate and Ilkley became Bettys and the tea and coffee importing and blending business was transferred here in 1971. Taylors' Yorkshire tea, one of the countries best selling brands has been produced here in Starbeck ever since.

The man who started it all. Frederick Belmont (born in Switzerland in 1883) with one of his hand crafted confectionery creations.

Built in 1922 on Prospect Road Starbeck. Bettys' Bakery was in full production until demolition at the beginning of the 21st century to allow for the expansion and improvements the new century demands.

Here we see the Confectionery team of around 1926. Most of the girls are unknown with the exception of Jessie Radcliffe seen here on the right. Jessie retired in 1981 after 55 years' service.

Another 1920s' picture, this time of the Bread and Pastry team in the original Bakehouse. The interior of the building remained almost unchanged until demolition in the summer of 2001

"Yes, darling, you may go to that party. I know they get all their things from Betty's."

Goods from Betty's are always of the finest quality, distinctive and reliable.

SHOP AT BETTY'S—THE HOUSE OF QUALITY.

Betty's Ltd Confectioners & Caterers

Another 1930s advert this time bearing the legend "Shop at Betty's-The House Of Quality".

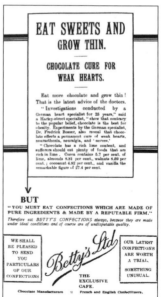

EAT SWEETS AND GROW THIN.

CHOCOLATE CURE FOR WEAK HEARTS.

Eat more chocolate and grow thin! That is the latest advice of the doctors. "Investigations conducted by a German heart specialist for 25 years," said a Harley-street specialist, "show that contrary to the popular belief, chocolate is the best for obesity. Experiments by the German specialist, Dr. Fredrick Busser, also reveal that chocolate effects a permanent cure of weak hearts, neurasthenia, neuralgia, and 'nerves.'

"Chocolate has a rich lime content, and sufferers should eat plenty of foods that are rich in lime. Cocoa contains 5.7 per cent, of lime, almonds 8.81 per cent, walnuts 8.69 per cent, ; cocoanut 4.82 per cent, and vanilla the remarkable figure of 27.4 per cent.

BUT
"YOU MUST EAT CONFECTIONS WHICH ARE MADE OF PURE INGREDIENTS & MADE BY A REPUTABLE FIRM."
Therefore eat BETTY'S CONFECTIONS always, because they are made under ideal conditions and of course are of undisputable quality.

WE SHALL BE PLEASED TO SEND YOU PARTICULARS OF OUR CONFECTIONS

Betty's Ltd

OUR LATEST CONFECTIONS ARE WORTH A TRIAL.

SOMETHING UNUSUAL

THE EXCLUSIVE CAFE.

Chocolate Manufacturers :: French and English Confectioners.

A 1930s' Bettys chocolate advert. I wonder what today's health conscious society would make of the "Eat Sweets and grow thin" or "Chocolate cure for weak hearts" boasts. How times have changed.

Pictured here in the original Bakehouse is Mark Raine, a Baker and long-standing Starbeck resident ready for a day's baking with a rather large bag of flour.

A wedding cake decorator painstakingly puts finishing touches to a wedding cake in the original Bakery.

One of Bettys' modern Chocolatiers busy creating white chocolate bears ready to be despatched to children nationwide.

An example of the attention to detail that has become a Bettys' trademark. Every foiled chocolate is hand polished.

Another baker, this time baking bread in the new Craft Bakery.

Members of staff proudly display the awards earned by the highly acclaimed new Craft Bakery.

The new Craft Bakery, which opened on Plumpton Park Starbeck on 12th July 2000 built to allow the continuation of past success.

Opening in 2001 opposite the new Bakery here we see Bettys' Cookery School. Here the employees learn the required skills necessary to sustain the highest of standards.

Inside the new Cookery School where staff from the five Bettys' branches around Yorkshire receive menu training.

All pictures courtesy Bettys of Harrogate

A Changing World

The development of a community demands improvements, and improvements demand change. Some things change for the better, while others just change forever. For that reason it is always sad to see an old familiar landmark disappear under the wrecker's ball. History, the study of the past, is a wonderful thing, but it must never be allowed to hold back the future.

At first glance it seems like these two 1920 views have not changed at all, but closer inspection reveals a little more. Harpers grocery shop with its Dutch style façade still intact and the remainder of what has for so long been Jackson's split into another two separate shops. You will also notice the Co-op still has it's side windows, while the shops opposite still have their original late 19th-century fronts and canopies. Notice also the white tiling on the front walls that was a feature of all the brick built houses and shops between Camwal Terrace and the Methodist Church. The young trees have mostly gone now choked by fumes from the busy A59. (S Abbott postcard collection)

There were once two fine large semi-detached houses originally known as Forest Villas next door to and up the hill from the school, the lower one later became known as Forest Grange. In this picture from 1900 are Elizabeth Holroyd (the lady who donated the water trough at Forest Lane Head) with her coachman Joseph Johnson outside Forest Villa, which after standing empty for a couple of years was demolished in the mid-1930s to make way for the houses of Highbank Grove. Forest Grange was later converted into a small private school but was demolished in 1983 to make way for the aptly named Forest Grange Close.
(Starbeck Museum)

This scene changed dramatically in the early 1920s when these 15 acres of open fields became the St Andrews Housing Estate. About 100 council houses were built here to meet the demands of the expanding local population in the years following the First World War. (Harrogate Advertiser)

Queen Farm was property of the Queen Hotel (now the Cedar Court) and stood opposite the St Andrews Estate until demolition about 1930 to make way for the present modern housing estate. The farmland, principally used to produce food for the hotel, was also occasionally used by the military as a campsite whenever the army came to town.
(Harrogate Advertiser)

With the exception of the railway company, Octavius Atkinson's structural engineering company on Prospect Road was Starbeck's largest ever employer. Responsible for the design, fabrication and erection of anything from garages to power stations all over the world Atkinson's produced quality work in Starbeck from 1938 until moving to more convenient premises at Flaxby Moor in 1990. Despite the state of the art facilities the recession of the 1980s and early 90s had already bitten deep and Octavius Atkinson and Sons closed down in the spring of 1993. The old factory was demolished during 1991 to be redeveloped by parent company Taylor Woodrow, and is now the site of Morrisons Supermarket and the nearby new housing estates. (Starbeck Museum)

Perhaps the single biggest loss to Starbeck during the 20th century was the Railway industry. Once one of the most important rail centres in the North of England, the decline that started with the closure of the locomotive sheds in 1959, ended in 1978 with the demolition of the old station and the goods facilities shown here. The main function of these buildings was as a trans-shipment shed where goods from all round Britain would be received in bulk, then unloaded and split up into smaller loads, to be despatched on separate trains to their final destinations. (J Rogers)

Harrison Hill House was one of the oldest houses in Starbeck and stood on Bogs Lane by the north-western side of the school playing field. After extensive renovation by the Addyman family in the late 19th-century, it was for many years the home of Jean Addyman. Originally a cottage by the side of a pre-turnpike packhorse route it was mercilessly demolished in 1994 to make way for Hillbank View. (E Clark)

The Highbridge area between Starbeck and Knaresborough was greatly altered during the early 1930s. The bridge itself was widened and both the World's End and the George Hotel (now the Yorkshire Lass) public houses were greatly altered. As is evident from the picture, the World's End was totally demolished and rebuilt. (Harrogate Advertiser)

To use its full and official title, The Starbeck Pleasure Grounds and Municipal Bowling Green, opened to the public, amid much pomp and ceremony on June 8th 1907. Though by now largely redundant, this land, on Spa Lane, was originally part of the gardens attached to the Prince of Wales spa baths (now the public swimming baths), when the visitors used it for exercise after taking the waters. The park was laid out for the princely sum of £200 and a bandstand was added at a further cost of £5. The park was stocked with many plants and shrubs, some of which can still be seen today, the bandstand was used by performing bands regularly and "the Park" as it came to be known was a popular and well used (if small) public garden. The park fell into disrepair after the death of the park-keeper in the 1950s and was soon after reduced to its present state. (S Abbott postcard collection)

The West Riding Police Mounted Section stables were built on the site of Belmont House (also known as Paddock House) in 1960. Built to accommodate up to eight horses it was arranged by the chief constable that it should only be used for greys. Despite the protests of the horse loving members of the local community the stables closed in March 1998. The stables and also deserted houses soon fell victim to vandalism and as a result were demolished in 2001. (S Abbott)

Another victim of vandalism was the Fabric Care Research Association's laboratories on Knaresborough Road. Opening in 1958 and closing around 1999, the building was demolished in 2002 to make way for the new Halfords' motor spares business. (S Abbott)

There were once five petrol stations between Forest Lane Head and Leyland Road. Over the last 30 years of the 20th century all but this one have closed. The Esso petrol station closed during Spring 2002 for a major facelift and reopened during the summer coupled with a Tesco supermarket. (S Abbott)

The ancient royal hunting park, Bilton Park was sold off in 1628 to form five separate farms. One of these farms was Bilton Hall Farm. Standing beyond the end of Bilton Hall Drive the building is rarely seen by anyone other than those on official business. After closure this old farmhouse was earmarked for demolition and redevelopment for housing in the year 2002. (S Abbott)

Here we have a collection of old press advertisements relating to long gone businesses that rose and then disappeared throughout the 20th century, reminding us of the days when there was a shop on every corner.

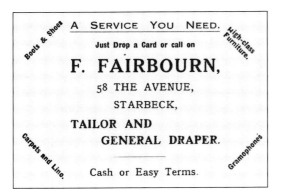

A SERVICE YOU NEED.

Boots & Shoes   High-class Furniture.

Just Drop a Card or call on

F. FAIRBOURN,

58 THE AVENUE,

STARBECK,

TAILOR AND

GENERAL DRAPER.

Carpets and Lino.   Gramophones.

Cash or Easy Terms.

WALLPAPERS

ADD CHARM TO THE HOME.

The Newest Patterns may be seen at

J. GREETHAM'S,

HOUSE DECORATOR,

61 High Street, Starbeck.

Eugene Permanent Waving.

Whole Shingled Head

from **30/-**

Perfection Guaranteed.

CYRIL BEER, 3 ALBERT PLACE
STARBECK.

Telephone : Knaresbro' **217**.

R. HEWSON,

Plumber, Glazier, Gasfitter,

and General Ironmonger,

15, BEECH STREET,

STARBECK.

Workshop : PROSPECT ROAD.

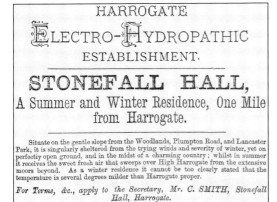

HARROGATE

Electro-Hydropathic

ESTABLISHMENT.

STONEFALL HALL,

A Summer and Winter Residence, One Mile from Harrogate.

Situate on the gentle slope from the Woodlands, Plumpton Road, and Lancaster Park, it is singularly sheltered from the trying winds and severity of winter, yet on perfectly open ground, and in the midst of a charming country ; whilst in summer it receives the sweet fresh air that sweeps over High Harrogate from the extensive moors beyond. As a winter residence it cannot be too clearly stated that the temperature is several degrees milder than Harrogate proper.

For Terms, &c., apply to the Secretary, Mr. C. SMITH, Stonefall Hall, Harrogate.

Telephone No. 107.   Telegrams : " Ice, Starbeck."

HARROGATE PURE ICE AND COLD STORAGE COMPANY,

LIMITED.

HIGH STREET, STARBECK, HARROGATE.

MANUFACTURERS OF PURE CRYSTAL ICE.

COLD STORAGE FOR GAME, MEAT, etc.

REFRIGERATORS ON SALE OR HIRE.

"CAMWAL"

(HARROGATE)

Table Waters

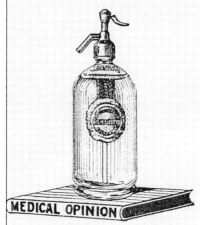

SODA WATER

POTASH WATER

LEMONADE

GINGER ALE

ORANGE CHAMPAGNE

Etc., Etc.

In Syphons or Bottles.

"CAMWAL" Dry Ginger Ale.

"CAMWAL" Brewed Ginger Beer

In Bottles or One Gallon Jars with Taps.

Harrogate Aquaperia

British Mineral Aperient Water,

Superior to all Foreign Waters.

CAMWAL HARROGATE LTD.

And at London, Manchester, Birmingham & Bristol.

Curiosities & Relics of Bygone Times

A look around the quiet corners in Starbeck today reveals many puzzling relics of the past, some ancient, some not so old. In this section we look at some puzzling photographs and the abundant remains of stones, buildings, and even gateposts that tell us of a history that in many cases requires a little explanation.

The venerable John Styan sits in his trap beside the old artesian well, which had supplied the neighbourhood with its fresh water until the community was connected to the mains during the 1870s. The well and a small reservoir were situated off what is now known as Prospect Road. (Harrogate Advertiser)

The large house at the very end of Forest Moor Road is most fondly remembered as Arlington House that was at one time the home of the Harrison family, one of whom was Miss Charlotte, the inspiration behind the Sunday school on Forest Lane that eventually evolved into St Andrews church. Still standing but mostly obscured from view we can see this old well just beside the house wall in the little wooded area next door. This well served the house and the farming community of the area around the bottom ends of Forest Lane, Hookstone Chase and Forest Moor Road. (S Abbott)

Though situated outside Starbeck this stone is a relic well worthy of inspection. Before the building of the turnpike roads and the enclosure of the Forest of Knaresborough in the late 18th century, the road system in the area was quite different to that we know today. The sharp corner where Rudding Lane bends around Rudding Park was once a busy junction where the roads from Knaresborough to Leeds and Spofforth to Harrogate crossed. Sometime after the road layout was changed an enterprising farmer moved the stone a short way along the road to be used as a gatepost. (S Abbott)

This stone stands beside the road on Forest Lane outside the children's football field. There is another where the two playing fields meet and a further one on Bogs Lane. Not long ago one was also found in the grounds of Springwater School. These are boundary stones dating from the forest enclosure of 1778 when for municipal reasons the new fields were designated detached parts of the townships to which the new landowners belonged. On one side of these stones is the letter K for Knaresborough, and on the other side SwT for Scriven with Tentergate.   (S Abbott)

This stone trough, now positioned at the top of Forest Lane near the Millfield housing estate, was a gift to the community, or rather a gift to the horses of the community, of Elizabeth Holroyd who lived at Forest Villa which once stood off the High Street between Starbeck School and Highbank Grove. Though some people claim it once stood beside the tollgate, (it was once positioned nearby), the date 1895 clearly disproves this as the tolls were abolished some 40 years previously. Elizabeth Holroyd was a great lover of animals and also endowed money to the school to be used to buy annual prizes for children who showed concern for animals. Miss Holroyd died in February 1904 and is buried in Grove Road cemetery. (S Abbott)

This gatepost stands at the entrance to Avenue Road and still bears some of the original fastenings. Built in the 1880s as a row of stylish houses known as Beech Grove Terrace, Avenue Road was originally a private road for residents only and was enclosed by a gate. It was opened up to the public during the late 1890s and early 1900s when the remainder of the houses were built. (S Abbott)

Thomas Addyman made his money supplying the army with leather boots, belts and straps during the Crimean War. He had moved to Starbeck in the 1850s, when he bought the estate belonging to the Williamsons which included most of the land in the triangle between Bogs Lane, Forest Lane and the railway lines. He built or refurbished most of Starbeck's more substantial houses. The family home, Belmont Villa, was probably the finest. Unfortunately all these houses are gone now, victims of later developers. All that remains of this once prominent and well-respected family is this solitary gatepost at the Northwest corner of what we still know as Addyman's Field.
(S Abbott)

This picture was taken one cold December morning in 1925 and shows the gate that stretched across the entrance to Bilton Hall Drive. The gate has now long disappeared but the picture reminds us, of the little known fact that Bilton Hall Drive and Bilton Lane are actually private roads, closed to non-residents' motor vehicles, but open as a footpath. Set out during mediaeval times as the road between Knaresborough and Old Bilton, Bilton Lane was downgraded as part of the enclosure act of 1778. (W Smith/Starbeck Museum)

Robert Johnson's greengrocery and confectionary shop where Camwal Road meets the High Street (now the laundrette). Mr Johnson took over the premises of the Starbeck branch of the Co-operative Society shop in February 1900 when the Co-op, having outgrown the shop, moved business to their present position at the junction of Forest Avenue and High Street. Robert Johnson remained here until 1947. In 1900 a Miss Carr, who for a short while ran a millinery business there, took the rear of the shop. (Starbeck Museum)

The former shop window of Miss Carr's millinery business behind Robert Johnson's shop (now the laundrette). This shop was entered by a door, now bricked up, just to the left of the window. Robert Johnson expanded his business to include this shop in 1903. (S Abbott)

This picture was taken around the 1930s/40s from what is now Wentworth Drive. Just visible between the trees is Belmont Villa (viewed here from the east) and nearby farm buildings. This picture also reminds us that as recently as the mid 1960s Addyman's Field was private and used for the grazing of cattle. (Starbeck Museum)

Two children play near Laundry Road just off The Avenue. Behind them is "The Lake". This stretch of water was the flooded remains of the Starbeck brickworks quarry at the end of Camwal Road. The brickworks closed down in the 1930s and the quarry was soon found to be dangerous, especially when full of water. The Harrogate Borough Council rectified the problem using the site as a landfill waste dump. Some local residents still refer to the area as "Tip Hill". The fact that the land was used as landfill has resulted in most of the area being unsuitable for building. (Starbeck Museum)

Opening in direct competition with the Starbeck Brickworks, was The Diamond Brick and Tile Company just a couple of fields away on Bogs Lane. The quarry to the rear has long since been filled in but the gatehouse remains and forms the office of a small building company yard. (S Abbott)

This fine beast guards the entrance to Shaw's Caravan Park on Knaresborough Road. Until recently there was a small water trough beneath it. This reminds us that throughout the middle of the 20th century the caravan park was the site of the Harrogate Agricultural Society Showground. The site also served as the home of the local football teams and tennis club. There was a single grandstand, which burned down and was never replaced. With the opening of the Yorkshire Showground on Wetherby Road the Starbeck showground closed and has became the site of Shaw's trailer park and for many years the local bank holiday funfair ground. (S Abbott)

Starbeck residents have travelled far and wide embracing customs and cultures all over the world. We here in Starbeck also open up our gates to visitors from so many places around the globe. This group came from the southern hemisphere and contribute to the modern farming activities that take place on the farmland that still surrounds Starbeck on almost all sides. (S Abbott)

During the later years of the 20th century many new words and phrases entered our vocabulary. One such term was 'global warming' and if these pictures from the winter of 1926 are anything to go by, then we certainly do have something to worry about. Here we see Schoolchildren huddled together to stave of the cold and damp of an autumn afternoon (left). As winter approached more than a foot of snow could fall overnight (opposite page top). On many occasions the river Nidd at Knaresborough would freeze enough to allow crowds to gather on the ice (opposite bottom).
(W Smith /Starbeck museum)

Dated 1955, this fine drawing of the old Belmont Cottages was the work of a member of the Addyman family and was found blowing around in the rubble after the cottages were demolished in the early 1970s. Erik Addyman's family grew up here in these old cottages that were also known locally as The White House. (Starbeck Museum)

Here is a collection of pictures of houses and buildings that most of us pass everyday, yet know so little about. In this section we have a look at some of our finest old buildings that are still on view, though not all are recognisable at first glance.

The lady of the house stands on the doorstep of "Clematis Lodge" whose name was derived from the fine clematis vines that grew around all sides giving the house a blaze of colour and a glorious aroma. The house, believed to be possibly 400 years old, is still there today (top right) at number 129 High Street, though in less picturesque surroundings and without the climbing clematis that gave it so much character. (Starbeck Museum)

The Lower High Street just before the turn of the 20th century was a familiar, yet different sight. Taken just before the 1904 rebuilding of the Star Inn this picture offers a good view of what was then Robert Hewson's plumbing and ironmongers shop that was demolished in the 1960s to make way for Reed's (now Staiano's) motorcycle shop. (S Abbott postcard collection)

This picture will get many people guessing, yet it is still there today in surroundings that are almost unchanged. This picture dates from 1910 when the house, standing on the right 150 yards up the hill towards Calcutt on Forest Moor Road, was the property of the Leeds Congregational Church who used the premises as a convalescent house for needy women parishioners. (S Abbott postcard collection)

Almost hidden by hedges, and sideways on to Forest Lane, just before Millfield Glade stands Butterfield Cottage. The house dates from the time of the forest enclosure and as is so obvious, takes its name from the fact that the adjacent field, now the first Forest Lane houses, was used for grazing cattle that produced milk for making butter. (S Abbott)

In 1380 John of Gaunt, Duke of Lancaster, ordered the building of a hunting lodge in Bilton Park. The lodge was built to replace an even earlier building that stood in the same grounds. This house, which is now known as Bilton Hall and serves as an excellent old peoples' home, is possibly the most historically important, and in parts the oldest, building in the borough. Having served for centuries as a royal hunting lodge, the deer park was sold off in 1628 and the hall became the seat of such illustrious families as the Slingsbys, who were stewards of the park and lived here from the 1550s to 1615, and their bitter rivals the Stockdales (1631-1742). At the beginning of the 20th century it was owned by Samuel Smith of Tadcaster brewery fame. Having much later been taken over by an engineering company who used the buildings as their national head office, it became a care home during the 1980s. Disappointingly, though much of the interior is original, the exterior was rebuilt during the 1850s, a time when the Victorians cared little for historical sentiment. (S Abbott)

The old stable block behind and adjoining Bilton Hall dates from the reign of Elizabeth I (1558-1603). (S Abbott)

Bogs farm, though the house is Victorian, (c 1860) dates back to the 17th century when it was formed as one of the original farms from the division of Bilton Park. This picture dates from the 1900s when the property was bought by the Chippindale family. Between them the Chippindale family have served Starbeck extremely well over the years. William Chippindale, who came to live on Forest Lane during the 1850s built the Stonefall and Starbeck brickworks and established the Starbeck saw mill that gave Camwal Road it's original name, Saw Mill Street. William's sons Amos and Arthur built many houses throughout Harrogate including most of those in the area of Diamond Place, Pearl Street and Regent Place and those at that end of the Avenue. The most famous of William Chippindale's sons though was James, another builder of many houses in the Harrogate area, who is most well known for his invaluable contribution to local politics, the pinnacle of which was becoming Mayor of Harrogate no less than three times. (Starbeck Museum)

To people around the country Harrogate has an image of snobbishness and this is a prime example of just how right they can be. When the demands of the early 19th century poor law called for a Harrogate workhouse, they built it here in Starbeck, so that the town's upper and middle class visitors would never notice that Harrogate had paupers. Now known as Starbeck Hall the workhouse opened in 1811 and ran until superseded by the Knaresborough union workhouse in 1858. Henry Peacock was the workhouse keeper here from 1825 to 1838 when he was sacked but went on to run the Brunswick Hotel (now the Prince of Wales Mansions) and serve as a Harrogate Improvement Commissioner. Since 1858 the building has been used as a private school, a hospice for people with incurable illnesses, a private home, offices for a firm of architects, and latterly apartments. (S Abbott)

The earliest houses to be built in the Starbeck area were around Forest Lane Head and this house at the junction with Maple Close is the oldest surviving. Originally built around 1700 as a farmstead known as Forest Lane Head Farm, within the last 40 years it has acquired the name Belmont House, not to be confused with the real house of that name that once stood opposite Starbeck Primary School. (S Abbott)

Another old farmhouse at Forest Lane Head is Pigeon Farm. The house was built in 1801, and stands facing Knaresborough Road at the very end of Bilton Hall Drive. After closure of the farm the buildings to the rear were converted into holiday chalets during the 1990s. The area we know as Forest Lane Head surprisingly predates the present Forest Lane and derives its name from the days when the road from the High Bridge was known as Forest Lane. (S Abbott)

Many houses were built on the green field sites between Starbeck and High Harrogate in the years between the two World Wars. This included the St Andrew's estate, all the houses between Roseville Road and Swarcliffe Road, and these along Kingsley Road. At the time of building (1926 – 27) a ditch of running water lay between the public footpath and the houses and every house was built with it's own little bridge. (Starbeck Museum)

This picture was taken just before the Second World War and shows the two Starbeck School buildings from the High Street at what is now the end of Avenue Close. Behind the gate are allotment gardens later to be occupied by the prisoner of war camp for the duration of the last war. After the war the empty camp buildings became a refuge for homeless couples that was known locally as the "Squatters Camp". An old peoples' care home was built here in 1968 but even that is now gone replaced by modern housing. (F Heaton)

A glimpse of a more fashionable past, these stables behind the Prince of Wales public house remind us that during the days of Starbecks Spa industry, this building was a hotel called the Spaw Inn, a popular resort for those who came to take the waters. (S Abbott)

Because of the length of this building and the narrowness of the back street on which it stands it is not easy to get a picture of this important piece of our industrial heritage. Though not particularly old, less than 100 years, this was between 1942 and 1957 the home of Hill's of Harrogate, makers of jam and other preserves. At other times a company of nameplate makers, engineering firms and a cabinet and upholstery company, have occupied the building. Since 1972 it has belonged to Robert Fell's plumbing and heating company. (S Abbott)

The houses at the corner of The Avenue and Victoria Terrace are pictured here around 1920 when the corner house was known as Wyndham House and was the home of J Kell who ran his grocery business here. They were built by the Chippindale brothers around about the turn of the century. Up to 1904 this end of The Avenue was known as Victoria Avenue and the Knaresborough Road end Albert Avenue, after the queen and her regent. (S Abbott postcard collection)

I wonder if we will grow to love this one as much. The new car showrooms were built behind the Henry Peacock public house at the end of the 20th century. During the later half of the 19th and first half of the 20th centuries William Tattersall's and later J P Simpson and Sons malt works occupied the site. It is marked on the 1854 OS maps as Starbeck Brewery. Just behind the brewery was the local artesian well and reservoir. (S Abbott)

Come Hell & High Water

It would be fair to say that Starbeck is not known for earthquakes, volcanoes, or hurricanes, but every now and then disaster strikes just when you least expect it. There was a famous horse drawn bus incident in 1903 and a runaway train crashed through the Starbeck gates during rush hour in 1972 but little else until.........

THE W(HOLE) TRUTH
Come to Harrogate, this famous spa,
People travel, from near and far,
The waters, pump rooms, Brimham Rocks,
Bring the tourists, in their flocks,
Then there's Mother Shipton's cave,
And Knaresboro' – That's all the rave,
The Stray, the flowers, and Yorkshire Show,
Makes Harrogate the place to go.
Now something new! And it's a mystery,
After telling you what's history,
A hole has come to Prospect Road,
They come to see it, by busload,
Starbeck has this new attraction,
Which has brought this great attraction.
It's just a hole – They've brought a digger,
But every week (the hole) gets bigger,
It's so deep – They employ miners,
They could flood it, and sail liners.
So if repairs become in vain?
They'll change it to a shipping Lane.

Alan Barker

All seemed well early one spring morning in 1998 as the Norbar staff arrived at the shop on Prospect Road. When unlocking the door one member of staff noticed signs of subsidence in the road outside. The authorities were alerted and Prospect Road was immediately cut off to vehicular traffic. By lunchtime excavations had started and news of what was to become known as "The Starbeck Hole", was spreading like wildfire. Initially it was a reasonably small hole and even the most outrageous estimates claimed that the remedial work would only take up to three weeks. (Norbar)

As the older members of the community were reminding everyone that the same thing had happened in the same place about 50 years previously, it was discovered that the cause was a mixture of loose moving sand and a broken water pipe. Sadly these pictures do the hole no justice, at the peak of its extent it was going on for 20m long, from outside Norbar almost to the white line in the centre of Knaresborough Road, taking in much of Prospect Park as it passed by. In the end Prospect Road and one lane of the High Street was closed for three very long months. (Norbar)

The hole is now almost refilled. All sorts of lorries and various pieces of plant equipment moved tonnes and tonnes of earth out and eventually back in. It was feared that all the buildings from Norbar to Blooms on the corner would have to be demolished, but luckily all those properties were saved. (Norbar)

SEQUEL TO THE (WHOLE) TRUTH

Prospect Road – is open now,
That hole it caused some fun,
To the workers one must bow.
Now the job's been done.

First they took out, tons of soil,
And many crowds it drew,
Some suggested… They'd struck oil,
One saw a….Kangaroo !!

Five months on … the work's complete,
New kerbs,…. And posh tarmac,
Now it looks like any street,
With folks….and traffic back.

Alan Barker

Monday 5th July 1999 had been a lovely sunny day until 3.15 pm when all of a sudden the sky turned black and the heavens opened up with a spectacular freak thunderstorm. The sudden influx of water was too much for the sewer that runs beside the railway track to take and within ten minutes the sewer had burst and forced the High Street tarmac up. By 4 o'clock there was something resembling a lake on both sides of the tracks. The cellars of the Henry Peacock pub, and all the shops at the bottom of the High Street filled with water and damage and lost stock amounted to tens of thousands of pounds' .

The rain had stopped and the day had returned back to 'tee shirt' weather when Andy Dean and John Dolphin arrived at the Henry Peacock, Eskimo style for their evening's refreshment. (Harrogate Advertiser)

The subway beneath the railway line was never going to be much of an obstacle for the thirsty Andy Dean and John Dolphin when opening time called. (Harrogate Advertiser)

For many Starbeck residents the trip home from work meant lengthy delays or rolling up the trouser legs and wading home. (Harrogate Advertiser)

Getting Around

A s we embark on the 21st century we see the demand for transport growing ever stronger. In the constant rush to get here and there we often wonder how we would have managed in days gone by.

When the 1751 Act of Parliament called for the improvement of the road network around the Harrogate District a turnpike road was laid from Boroughbridge to Harrogate passing through Knaresborough and Starbeck. The building of the road itself was the work of the famous John Metcalf; otherwise know as "Blind Jack of Knaresborough", the remarkable man included road building in his impressive list of achievements. Tollhouses were built at junctions along the way including this one that is still standing at the top of the hill, to collect tolls at the junction with Bogs Lane.

Two hundred and fifty years later the tollhouse is still there though it is around 150 years since it has collected a toll.   (S Abbott)

Pictured at the beginning of the 20th century, a horse and cart stand outside the Harrogate Hotel (Now the Henry Peacock). In the background the early railway buildings before the erection of the trans-shipment sheds during the 1920s. Starbeck was then a bustling railway community with a busy station and in those days before the advent of the motorcar, taxi trade between Starbeck and Harrogate was booming for anyone with a horse and cart and a mind for business. (Starbeck Museum)

This 1912 picture shows the driver, with his young conductor and a full load of passengers waiting at the Starbeck terminus while the water tank of his Clarkson open topped double decker steam bus is topped up from the nearby hydrant. In the background, the signal box, subway and old station canopy can be seen. (Starbeck Museum)

Early morning in 1904, there are already a number of people about but very little traffic as this solitary horse and cart makes it's way towards the level crossing. (S Abbott postcard collection)

An early morning in the year 2000 and the scene is very different. Despite continuous calls for a bypass, which began as early as 1849, the main Knaresborough to Harrogate road just gets busier and busier. (S Abbott)

The Atora Suet wagon pulled by a team of oxen rolls past the Belmont Cottages during the inter war years. (Starbeck Museum)

This 1926 picture shows school caretaker William Smith and son Walter, a young girl and a dog, getting around in another irregular form of transport. Walter Smith would succeed his father as caretaker in 1931. The wall in the background ran between the two school buildings dividing the playground into two halves. (W Smith/Starbeck Museum)

One of Erik Addyman's Zephyr gliders pictured here outside the billiard room of Belmont Villa where he did much of his work. Erik Addyman was a pioneer of many revolutionary engineering projects of both powered and unpowered flight. His wife was the country's first lady glider pilot and at nine years old his son Oscar was the youngest. (Starbeck Museum)

These pictures show one of Erik Addyman's Vortex motorcars designed and handbuilt in Starbeck by the man himself. A car similar to this one was once damaged on the drive to Belmont Villa and as a result bricked in to the back wall of Mr Addyman's garage where it was almost forgotten until being "rediscovered" in the late 1960s. (Starbeck Museum)

For some the old forms of transport are the best. There are many stables and riding schools around the Forest Lane, Bogs Lane, and Bilton Hall Lane areas, and many public bridleways, like this one along the old Leeds and Thirsk railway line, to serve the needs of the equestrians amongst us. (S Abbott)

The 20th Century High Street
A Walk Through Starbeck in the Year 1900

We start our 1900 tour at Forest Lane Head, outside the recently laid out golf course. This area is still a part of the borough of Knaresborough and will remain so until the local boundaries are adjusted just before the Second World War. From here we see Pigeon Farm at the entrance to Bilton Hall Lane and Forest Lane Head Farm opposite. Set back a little off the road we see a group of houses that we know as "Taylortown" due to the high percentage of residents with that name. A little further on we find Forest Hill House and the little café belonging to Miss Robson. As we approach Crimple Lane (now Forest Lane), we pass the track that leads to Millfield House, 50 years ago there was a windmill here, nowadays goats graze in the mill field.

Crossing the Crimple Lane we now enter the borough of Harrogate. To our right we see the old Toll House that was built to take the tolls when "Blind Jack" built this road back in the 1750s. Next to that we see Clematis Lodge and then Forest Villa and Forest Grange. On the left is Grove Cottage (or The Grove), the home of Mr Daniel Atkinson. The little statue in his garden is of Grace Darling, it is said that he is somehow related to her. Below The Grove we have the extensive gardens of Belmont House, the oldest of our grander houses. Soon the Vicarage will be built here and then after the demolition of Belmont House in 1957, stables and housing for the police force and Springwater school. For now though let us admire the fine gardens stretching from The Grove right down to Belmont Cottages. These cottages will be demolished in the early 1970s but for now they stand by the entrance to Belmont Villa, another grand house. Opposite Belmont House (later known as Paddock House) is the new council school that was built in 1896. Next to the school is an area of allotment gardens; during the 1940s this will become a prisoner of war camp. From here, in the distance, you can just see Harrison Hill House standing set back off Bogs Lane.

Opposite the end of Albert (now The) Avenue we have Addyman's Field and at the top of the field Belmont Villa. This is the home of the Addyman family, the prominent local family. After the field is the little St Andrews chapel built in 1889 as a chapel of ease for Christ Church. Soon that will be coming down and in 10 years we will have a big new church here. Opposite St Andrews, at the junction of Albert Place and the High Street we have the Primitive Methodist Church. This too will come down, but not until after union with the Wesleyans and the new Methodist Church is built opposite Addyman's field in 1931.

Now we come to the local shopping area. The Prince of Wales public house was built as the Spaw Inn around the middle of the 19th century. Opposite the Prince we have the site of the new Co-operative stores. They have outgrown their original shop at the end of Saw Mill Street (now the laundry at the end of Camwal Road). Behind the old Co-op is Camwal's mineral water plant.

At the very bottom of the hill just before the railway station we have a number of shops and then Old Beck Street while on the other side are the railway cottages and the old Star Inn. This is a very old inn and during the next year or so it will be torn down to be turned into a new and much larger Star Inn, which is due to open in 1904.

Then we have the railway station and behind that goods and coal yards. Across the road behind the Harrogate Hotel (now the Henry Peacock), and Tattersall's Malt works we have the engine shed and shunting yards. The railways are the lifeblood of our community; most of the local men work here.

As we pass the end of Prospect Road where lots of new houses have just been built, and head for Beech Grove Terrace, a private road with a gate, (now Avenue Road) we also pass Beech Cottage to our right (the site of Ravenscourt) the former home of John Turner. Above that are some fine houses and then the old workhouse. The old workhouse was a school not so long ago, but at the moment it is Mr CH Winter's home for chronic diseases. Opposite the workhouse at the end of Stonefall Terrace, we have Atkinson's Corn Mill; this thoroughly modern mill is powered by steam and has put the old windmill at Forest Lane Head out of business, but alas, this place is due for closure, but not to worry it will soon become our very own ice factory.

Pictured here in 1900 is the original Star Inn building. This inn dated from around the time of the forest enclosure of 1778. It was demolished in 1903 and replaced with the far bigger and smarter building, which opened in 1904 and served the community until closure in the 1950s when it's liquor licence was transferred to the Broad Acres (now The Mapplebeck). Having then been home to Christine's bakery for many years the building now hosts a furniture and carpet shop. (Harrogate Advertiser)

A closer look at the cottages (38-46 High Street) that stood next to the original Star Inn and were pulled down at the same time. To the left of the cottages is the block of shops 48 to 54 High Street under construction. This dates the picture in the mid 1890s (Starbeck Museum)

A lonely horse and cart makes its way up the High Street towards Knaresborough in the early 1900s. The two young boys and a lady are standing at the corner of The Avenue. A passing dog takes a canine interest in the trees. A hundred years later traffic congestion would become a major problem. (S Abbott postcard collection)

A familiar view of the High Street. A horse and cart passes the Prince of Wales heading towards Knaresborough. Other historians have dated this picture as 1910. The Co-operative store of February 1900 is there but the chemist shop next door of 1904 has yet to appear. Therefore the picture was taken between 1900 and 1904. (S Abbott postcard collection)

Another High Street picture of a similar date this time looking from the end of Stonefall Avenue towards the railway crossing. These pictures give Starbeck a quiet and undisturbed look. With all the railway activity and other industries going on nearby this is something of a false impression. The steam corn mill (just off picture to the right) was particularly noisy. (S Abbott postcard collection)

An early motorist stops to talk to a cyclist in a picture dated 1912. The picture was taken from the forecourt of The Harrogate Hotel (now The Henry Peacock) looking towards Harrogate. To the right are the coal yard office and a small brick railway building. The railway company would soon redevelop this land building a large trans-shipment shed here. It is now the site of the Station View complex. (S Abbott postcard collection)

This picture shows the gatehouse/lodge of Belmont Villa. It was pulled down in the early 1970s together with the nearby Belmont cottages to make way for the extension of Springwater School and the adult centre for work, education and social training. (Starbeck Museum)

Belmont Villa. This was the home of the Addyman family. Built in the 1860s to a design by the same architect who built the Victoria Baths (now the Municipal Offices) it was demolished in 1968 to make way for a dual carriageway that was intended to bypass the railway crossing. The fine house was ruthlessly demolished, but we still await the by-pass. (Starbeck Museum)

Here we see Belmont Cottages also known as The White House. These stood by the High Street opposite the Methodist church. Some estimates dated them as early as 17th century. In the yards behind was a linen dying tank, evidence that they had at one time been used in the linen industry. From 1927 until demolition they had been the home of Erik Addyman and his family. (Starbeck Museum)

The Starbeck Board School. This picture was taken during or just before First World War. Note the tree and garden where the war memorial of 1923 now stands. (S Abbott postcard collection)

This photograph, taken in the 1900s is of Albert Winterburn outside his butchers shop at no 57 High Street. This was Mr Winterburn's third shop having previously run his business from just around the corner on Albert Place, and the shop next door to this one. Number 57 High Street is now Jervis' lighting and gift shop. (Starbeck Museum)

Clematis Lodge, at number 129 High Street is believed to be up to 400 years old. This house is still standing and still more or less in its original form, although the surroundings have changed dramatically. (Starbeck Museum)

A view of the High Street taken in 1920. This view is interesting because it shows a clear view of Cawood's bakery and confectioners seen here advertising Fry's chocolate, and Lockwood's second-hand furniture shop, on the site now occupied by Stiano's motorcycle business. Cawood's was later Broadbents and then Holden and Kassell's Star bakery. Later on it was local councillor Jack Blakey's electrical store. The Lockwood brothers also had another shop on the other side of the road along with the local scrap metal dealership. (S Abbott postcard collection)

In this 1930s' scene, proudly standing at the door of the second Star Inn building are the landlord and landlady Mr and Mrs Boyce. Though this is not a very clear photograph it is still possible to make out the ornamental stonework and stained glass windows. The building, though now almost 50 years since closure, still advertises Warwick's of Boroughbridge Celebrated Ales and Stout. (Starbeck Museum)

Here we see the Starbeck Police House and Office. These and the police mounted section stables behind having opened in 1960, occupied the land directly opposite Starbeck Primary School. The stables closed in March 1998 and the site was levelled for redevelopment during 2001.
(S Abbott)

Two more of the Police houses. At the time of construction all new built police houses around the country were built to exactly the same design. This allowed transferred officers to take their carpets and furniture with them. (S Abbott)

This picture taken from the end of Kingsley Road in the 1900s shows an avenue of fine trees. During the 19th century this area was known as Beech Grove. The trees were all chopped down for safety reasons in the 1950s after one was brought down during heavy gales. (Starbeck Museum)

A 1930s view this time of the other end of Beech Grove looking from the end of Stonefall Avenue. To the right is the entrance to the old Workhouse. (S Abbott postcard collection)

Photographed in its present form this is the 18th-century tollhouse that stood to take tolls on the Harrogate to Boroughbridge turnpike road built by John "Blind Jack" Metcalf in the 1750s. The house was sited here to cover the crossroads with Forest and Bogs Lanes. (S Abbott)

Later known as Paddock House, the 18th-century Belmont House was the earliest of Starbeck's finest houses. Situated opposite Starbeck School it was the home of many prominent local families. Having served for 10 years as the nurses' home for the General Hospital, this splendid house was demolished in 1958 to make way for Springwater School and the police houses and stables. (Starbeck Museum)

The spirit of any place is created by its people. The characters that live among us give this community its own special atmosphere. Over the years Starbeck has produced many unique and talented people, many of them are mentioned in other sections of this book.

A well-remembered local character Samuel St Paul sets off on his rounds with his milk churn and bottles on his handlebars. He delivered milk in this way around the streets of Starbeck for many years. He owned the dairy at 71 High Street from 1928 until 1958 when the business was passed on to his stepson John Clemmitt. The shop was always known as "The Dairy" right up to its eventual closure in the late 1970s when owner Harry Davy, who took over the shop in 1972, closed for business and the building reverted back to a private house. (Starbeck Museum)

Opposite far left: The man in the picture is Walter Smith, Starbeck Primary School caretaker throughout the middle and latter half of the 20th century, who took over from his father in 1931. This interesting late 1920s picture shows him as a younger man with his "Meccano" clock that he constructed himself in 1926. He was also quite an accomplished photographer easily mastering all the latest techniques. (Starbeck Museum)

Opposite near left: This 1924 picture shows Albert Winterburn (left) and Billy Wise (right) the tallest and shortest members of the Starbeck Working Men's Club. Mr Winterburn ran a successful butchery business near the post office and Mr Wise worked at the Camwal water bottling plant. (Starbeck Working Men's Club)

Opposite bottom, left & right: Amateur dramatic societies have long been established in Starbeck and here is one of the stars of the shows during the 1930s. Bob Scales was well known for his singing talents and is pictured here as a star of Ruddigore (opposite bottom left) in which he appeared at the Royal Spa rooms (next to the Royal hall) in November 1936 and The Mikado at the same venue in 1938. For his living Bob Scales ran a kitchen garden, which he had taken over from his father, that was situated beside the upper school building where the houses of Hillbank Grove stand today. Sadly Bob Scales died in 1947 at the tragically young age of 34. (Starbeck Museum)

Not really a natural born Starbeckian this is HRH Princess Mary (later the Princess Royal) laying the foundation stone of the Harrogate General Hospital on Knaresborough Road, 3rd September 1926. (Harrogate Advertiser)

Miss Jessie Dean, who once resided on Regent Place, along with a Miss Bullock had the distinction of being the first members of the Women's section of the Leeds City police force having previously served in the Metropolitan force. This photograph shows her at her work on the day she became the first female police officer to achieve the rank of Chief Inspector, November 1955. (Starbeck Museum)

Life for children all over Europe was never easy during the 1940s and this group of Starbeck schoolchildren with hoops and footballs had taken the opportunity to put the hardships behind them with sports activities in the school playground. Many of these children still live in the area 60 years later. Back L to R: Margaret Pratt, Frank Heaton, Dorothy Pyne (whose uncle ran the coach company), Michael Todd, Mary Pearce.

Front L to R: Pamela Middleton, Joan Rhodes, Doris Sugden, Joyce Hartley, Muriel Atkinson, Joyce Carrick.   (Frank Heaton)

A remarkable member of a remarkable family. This is Erik Addyman, son of James Addyman Vice Consul to Norway. Erik Addyman could only be described as a mathematical and mechanical genius. He designed and built his own motorcars and aircraft (both powered and gliders). He designed engines and components that were simply years ahead of their time. He ran the Harrogate aircraft club and was the prominent party in the 1930s' campaign to provide Harrogate with a municipal airfield at Rudfarlington. His sons have all achieved great things in their own right. Oscar rose to colonel in the army before embarking on a remarkable career as a civil engineer, James was a mechanical engineer and youngest son Peter is a prominent archaeologist and as director of the York Archaeological Trust is responsible for the famous Yorvik centre. (Starbeck Museum)

Erik Addyman and another enthusiast in a storeroom at Belmont Villa working on parts of an Addyman Zephyr glider. (Starbeck Museum)

Starbeck Coal Yard May 1973. Derek Henderson, Ray Cobley and owner Richard Clifford who ran the business beside the old railway yards on the west side of the Knaresborough Road. (Moyra Osborne)

Teaching the Children

With the rapid growth of Starbeck in the latter half of the 19th century came children and the need for schools. The old workhouse had been a private boys school for 20 years from 1860 to 1880, but the majority of Starbeck children had to walk to High Harrogate or Knaresborough for their education if they were taking it at all. In the 1890s two temporary schools opened. One was very limited by size and was situated on The Avenue, the other was St Andrew's school on Forest Lane. Eventually Starbeck Board School opened in 1896 to be followed later by the private Forest Grange School, then in the 1960s by Hookstone Chase Primary.

This building is of course the old workhouse, built during 1810 and 1811. The workhouse closed in 1858 and in 1860 became the Beech Grove Academy, a private school for around 30 boys under the tuition of T W Sawyer. The school closed when lessons were transferred to Victoria Avenue in Harrogate in 1880. The building went on to become a hospice for incurables, a private residence by the name of Old Starbeck Hall, offices for a company of architects and finally modern apartments. (S Abbott)

Pictured here around 1910 Starbeck Board School was built in 1895 and opened for lessons in the early summer of 1896. The building to the left of the school is the caretaker's house and to the right the headmaster's living quarters. In place of the war memorial is an ornamental garden and a placard advertising evening art and technical classes for adults. Other than the 1923 addition of the war memorial, the scene is little changed from that we know today. (Starbeck Museum)

However new and up to date, the School soon proved inadequate and in 1903 this building was built. Initially it formed the infant school but was soon sensibly changed to accommodate the older children. It remained as Starbeck Secondary School until the opening of Granby Park School in 1965. (S Abbott)

Under the watchful eye of headmaster Richard Roberts, the young boys, momentarily put the troubles of the ongoing First World War behind them and engage in a game of football. The pitch on this occasion is in the top right hand corner of the playground between the upper school and what was the bicycle sheds. Behind them and possibly being used as goalposts we see exercise apparatus. (Starbeck Museum)

Judging by the expressions on the faces of these two classes, school around the year 1910 was anything but enjoyable. (Starbeck Museum)

For this picture taken around 1912 we have an almost complete line up.

(Back row left to right), Harry Smith, George Readman, Ivor Henderson, Jimmy Race, Arthur Kemp, Harry Stocking, Wilf Brown, Harry Dickenson.

(4th Row L to R) Richard Clifford, Bell, Mills, Marion Grosvenor, Elsie Howston, Pybus, Ivy Lister, Maisie Lancaster, Alice Birchill, R Langley, Frank Swift, unknown, Stuart McDonald. (3rd row L to R) Reg Castledine, Jim Metcalf, Gladys Whitehouse, Phyllis Atkinson, Lucy Hargreaves, unknown, Hilda Hogg, Connie Bradley, unknown, Lucy Taylor, Freda Middleton, Emily Bramley.

(2nd row L to R) Herbert Howard, Edgar Higginson, Tom Walker, Fred Cooper, E Rawlinson, Ted Simpson, Francis Walker, Willie Clarke, Hugh Sleight, Fred Macow, Cecil Winter, (Front row L to R) Harry Boston, Frank Burns, Harry Langton, Willie Wetherill. (M Osborne)

Mr William Smith. The school owes a great debt to William Smith and his son Walter who gave the school around 100 years service as caretakers. William was the first school caretaker from 1896 to retirement in 1931 when his son Walter took over and remained until his own retirement in the late 1980s. Walter was also a keen photographer and his skill can be seen in many of these pictures that were donated to the museum. (W Smith/Starbeck Museum)

Children play in the side playground on a red-hot day during the summer of 1926. The interesting feature of this picture is over the wall where we see vegetables growing in the allotments where the Second World War prison camp/Starbeck house old peoples home/modern houses would be built in the forthcoming years. (W Smith/Starbeck Museum)

Judging by the piano and pictures, this otherwise empty 1926 classroom, was used for music and religious studies. (W Smith/Starbeck Museum)

The infant school hall in August 1925. Looking from the back of the hall towards the headmaster's office, reception and the entrance doors, this view has changed very little over the years. Clearly visible on their long cables are the recently installed, original electric lights. The two school buildings were more than likely the first buildings in Starbeck to have electric lights. In both buildings the lights were operated by a key to which only the headmaster had access. (W Smith/Starbeck Museum)

Sitting front right is Mr James the school attendance officer. It was his job throughout the 1920s and 1930s to ensure the children attended school. Rounding up the truants was an unenviable task that earned him the nickname "kid catcher". (Starbeck Museum)

Sat front centre in this 1929 staff photograph is headmaster TW Gray who was the second headmaster of Starbeck School taking over from Richard Roberts in 1926 and serving until 1943 when he was succeeded by Mr Lance Crosby. (Starbeck Museum)

This staff picture was taken about the time of the outbreak of World War Two. Front row is L to R, Miss Smailes, unknown (possibly miss Wrack), Miss Atkinson (who married Mr Powell), Miss Hay, Miss Ferguson, Miss Broadbent, Miss Wright. Back Row L to R, Mr Bissett, Mr Sandy Powell, Mr T W Gray (head), Mr Harris, Mr Mumford, Mr Stirling. (Starbeck Museum)

Judging by the positioning and the fact that the lady teacher sat front central (Miss Smailes) is wearing the same dress it is a fair assumption that this class photograph was taken on the same day as the last picture. (Starbeck Museum)

By the time this picture of Form 2A was taken in 1947, teacher Miss Atkinson had married a colleague and become Mrs Powell. The full line up is, Back row L to R, N Lomax, P Dodsworth, B Lawrence, B Barker, K Lockwood, B Plummer. 3rd Row S Carrick, J Clifford, J Sissons, J Outhwaite, Mrs Powell, B Boddy, N Hespin, N Robshaw, E Boyd. 2nd row W Yates, J Rogers, B Whitehouse, C Murgatroyd, P Ashburner, M Kent, J Cundall, T Wilson, J Wrigglesworth. Front row E Lofthouse, D Barnard, B Ascough, S Patrick, D Lupton, P Dennis, N Simpson, E Dunne. (Starbeck Museum)

The all conquering Starbeck school first eleven of the 1947-48 season pictured with both the local schools cups. Back row L to R: B Outhwaite, D Swift, G Dunnington, P Spruce, C Court. Middle row: M Gotts, C Bentley, D Pool. Front: W Everitt, W Thompson, P Roberts. (Starbeck Museum)

These two 1950s' pictures show the pupils well behaved and quietly working in the reading corner and the art room. The boys are dressed in short trousers and ties and the girls in pinafores and ribbons, a far cry from today's youth fashions. (Starbeck Museum)

The Johnson twins with their drums lead the Starbeck Primary School band in 1960.
(Starbeck Museum)

Everything seems to have grown as we see Mr and Mrs Elliott with the Starbeck Primary School
Orchestra in 1980 (Starbeck Museum)

Mrs Powell's class of 1980. (Starbeck Museum)

Just over the wall from Starbeck Primary School was Forest Grange School. This was a small private school for a limited number of pupils, which ran from 1960 until closure and demolition in 1983. Originally a fine private house, the building was knocked down to make way for the present houses of the aptly named Forest Grange Close. In this 1983 picture we see the Headmistress, Mrs Kathleen Harrison surrounded by the final year's teachers and pupils. (Starbeck Museum)

With happy smiles and their whole futures ahead of them, on the entrance steps are the Starbeck Primary School new starters of 1992. (Harrogate Advertiser)

To celebrate the centenary of Starbeck Primary School on Friday 7th June 1996 the school held a special day of celebration with all the children attending the festivities dressed in Victorian Clothes. Roxanne Hunter poses here with brother James and friend Amy Foster. (S Abbott)

The retirement of longstanding "Lollipop" lady Mrs Sandra Cremins was marked with a special assembly in April 2002. Mrs Cremins, who had taken care of the children on the busy Knaresborough road for 21 years, was presented with a bouquet of flowers at the assembly attended by all pupils and teachers. The road directly outside the school is one of the busiest in the district and a crossing attendant had been used for many many years. However after failing to find a suitable candidate the Harrogate Borough Council replaced Mrs Cremins with a Pelican Crossing. (Harrogate Advertiser)

There was a lot of house building at the lower end of Forest Lane during the 1950s and 60s. This led to the need for a new school resulting in the demolition of Oak Farm and the building of Hookstone Chase primary in the mid to late 1960s. Hookstone is a fine school with an excellent reputation. In this picture from May 2002 the youngsters have been enjoying some special football coaching from the experts. Pictured with the kids are Paul Atkinson and Miles Sutton of Leeds United AFC. (Harrogate Advertiser)

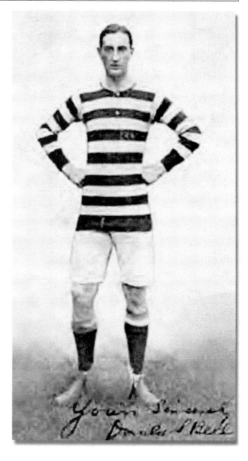

DONALD SIMPSON BELL VC was the star of the Starbeck Football Club as they dominated local football in the early 1900s, this all-round athlete eventually found himself playing professional football at Bradford Park Avenue FC. At the same time he went through university and was appointed assistant master at Starbeck School. Shortly after the outbreak of hostilities he joined the Green Howards and quickly rose through the ranks until he reached 2nd Lieutenant. During the summer of 1916 he was in France and found himself taking part in the Battle of the Somme. One morning his battalion was ordered to leave its position and capture "Horseshoe Trench". Immediately they came under deadly fire from an enemy machine gun. On his own initiative 2nd Lieutenant Bell led two other men along a communication trench and across open ground. From around 20 yards he hit the gun first throw with a grenade and knocked it out and in doing so saved the lives of many of his battalion. Five days later he was again in action around the village of Contalmaison. While leading his men past the barricades to protect their position he was killed. The spot on which he died was officially named Bell's Redoubt. A few short days later September 9th 1916 he was posthumously awarded the Victoria Cross on for his actions at Horseshoe Trench.

The sadness and respect can be seen in their faces as Donald Bell's widow reads letters from her husband to some of his pupils in the schoolyard shortly after his death. To this day inside the entrance to the school is a memorial plaque in commemoration of 2nd Lieutenant D S Bell. (Starbeck Museum)

For many years after his death young boys would daily pay their respects to D S Bell by saluting a photograph in the playground every morning. This idea was instigated by the headmaster Mr Richard Roberts' who served the school from its opening in January 1895 to retirement in December 1925. (Starbeck Museum)

Private A Wells of 14 Albert Terrace (now Camwal Terrace) was severely wounded during the fighting around Neuve Chapelle, and was sent back to England for treatment at Clacton-on-Sea and Middlesex Hospitals where he died of his wounds. Shortly after his death he was given a full military funeral with a cortege from the family home to his burial at the Grove Road cemetery. (Harrogate Advertiser)

The cenotaph was unveiled in Starbeck in the spring of 1923. Here at one of the first remembrance services we see the mood of the people as they brave the wet and cold November weather to pay their respects to the 100 names on the roll of honour. (Starbeck Museum)

This is a picture of Francis West vicar of St Andrew's from 1938 to 1942. He was called up as a military chaplain soon after the outbreak of the Second World War and returned only briefly to recover from wounds he suffered in Belgium during action leading up to Dunkirk. He resigned the living in 1942.
(Starbeck Museum)

The membership of Starbeck Working Men's Club (apart from those serving), gather outside the club on VE day 1945. Behind the group, bunting is going up for the peace celebrations. (SWMC)

Members of the local Home Guard and Air Raids Precaution units shortly after the war are pictured receiving awards from their commanding officers. (Starbeck museum)

All over the country celebrations were held as the world began to recover from six years of hostilities. Every street had a party of its own. Here we see the happy children of Starbeck and their parents. Such happy days had been a long time coming and all contributed to the festivities. (Harrogate Advertiser)

The crowds gather and local dignitaries stand to attention as the Remembrance parade of 1959 reaches the cenotaph. For some unknown reason this would be the last remembrance day parade until the services resumed 30 years later in 1989. (Starbeck Museum)

The Starbeck War Memorial was built in 1923 by Harrogate building firm F Hymas. By the 1980s it had fallen into disrepair and was looking neglected. A group of local people including Gordon Beer, local councillor Jack Blakey and school headmaster David Hardcastle made attempts to find out who was responsible and to have the situation rectified. Eventually it was discovered that the memorial and land was given to an unknown society in 1920 that no longer existed. Eventually the council, led by Mr Blakey, took the matter to hand and restored the cenotaph. Armistice services resumed in November 1989. (Photo S Abbott)

The restoration works were finished off in time for the year 2000 service with the replacement of the railings taken down in the early 1940s to provide much needed scrap metal as part of the national war effort. The replacement railings were copies of the originals and pictured here we see Mayor of Harrogate and Starbeck Councillor Pat Marsh, Mike Hine who organised the new railings with Nigel Parry who organises the annual service. (Harrogate Advertiser)

Three Starbeck councillors pictured at the 1995 remembrance service. Pat Marsh (Chairman of Leisure and Amenities), Barry Haxby (Mayor), and Phillip Broadbank Chairman of Housing); all three would stand as Harrogate Mayor during the 1990s. (Pat Marsh)

The 1993 Remembrance service. Mr Sample lays a wreath on behalf of Starbeck Working Men's Club under the watchful eyes of both the young and old. (Starbeck Museum)

At the bottom of Forest Lane we have the Stonefall cemetery home of the Commonwealth War Graves Commission. Here we have the graves of the brave young airmen who lost their lives during the Second World War from the air bases all over Yorkshire. Along with RAF men, here lie many casualties from Canada, New Zealand and Australia. (S Abbott)

A Community That Cares

So many years after the closure of the spa facilities, Starbeck goes on caring for the elderly and the less fortunate amongst us. There is a college for the blind, Springwater School for handicapped children, two facilities for handicapped adults and numerous old peoples homes, and complexes. Due to the vulnerability of some of the people at these establishments, it was requested that pictures and details be kept to a minimum.

Situated in the quietest of corners is Henshaw's college for the education and training of the blind on Bogs Lane. This thoroughly modern facility was opened by HRH the Duchess of Kent on 23rd November 1971, since which time it has provided care and training of the highest standards. (S Abbott)

Providing a special education for pupils with special needs, Springwater School opened on the High Street during the 1960s. The specialist teaching staff offer children from 2 to 19 years, education and training tailored to suit their individual needs. Specialist provision is made for hydrotherapy and a full range of sensory facilities are available including a woodland walk. Physiotherapy, occupational therapy, and speech and language therapy are included to offer the pupil the most up to date methods to improve their quality of life and independence. (S Abbott)

The Harrogate General Hospital that opened in 1938 to relieve the overcrowding of the Harrogate Infirmary (now St Peter's school). Having served the Harrogate area for 60 years the hospital was phased out during the 1990s as treatment was gradually transferred to the new Harrogate District Hospital further up Knaresborough Road. The 1930s' buildings were demolished over 1999 and 2000 and the site is currently being redeveloped as a modern housing complex.

The present Ravenscourt residential home for the elderly was built during the 1980s to replace the earlier building that was once known as Castle Villa and before that Beech Cottage, home of the redoubtable John Turner. (S Abbott)

After the demolition of the Starbeck north yard railway facilities the Station View complex was opened in the early 1980s to provide care for the elderly. (S Abbott)

A Spa Of Our Own

Many historians have written endlessly about the miraculous waters that formed the very foundation of Harrogate as one of the world's leading health resorts throughout the 18th and 19th centuries. One thing all these writers have in common is that they all give no more than a passing mention to the waters of Starbeck. Yet Starbeck had a thriving spa industry all of its own. They do not like to admit that the milder Starbeck waters were famous as a cure for some complaints that the harsher Low Harrogate sulphur water only aggravated, any more than they admit that Starbeck was home to the district's first purpose-built public bathing establishment.

During the latter half of the 16th century two mineral springs were discovered at Starbeck, one of mild sulphur and the other of chalybeate. When Michael Calvert inspired the people of Knaresborough in 1822 to refurbish the Starbeck Old Spa, which had fallen victim to sabotage and neglect, Starbeck was then technically still a part of Knaresborough. The results of this were the building of a bathhouse (right) and keeper's cottage (centre) in 1823 that bore the name Knaresborough Spaw. The waters, both chalybeate and sulphur once again became very popular. Not only was it soon discovered that the milder Starbeck sulphur water cured some skin conditions that the low Harrogate waters only aggravated, but it was also quickly evident that they lacked the off-putting taste and odour of their more illustrious rivals.

By the 1840s the Starbeck wells had become so popular that it soon became necessary to redevelop in order to cope with the increased demand due to the arrival of the railways and the discovery of a further chalybeate and two more sulphur springs. The cottage was demolished and this fine building that we know today as Spa Mews was opened in 1848.

In 1868 another sulphur spring was discovered in a field adjacent to the original springs. This led to the building of a rival establishment and a bitter feud that would all but destroy both. The Prince of Wales Baths opened in direct competition to the original in 1870. Along with a full range of water treatments the Prince of Wales company also boasted the Harrogate area's first ever swimming pool. Matching the neighbouring establishment the baths provided service to around 400 visitors daily. The building still stands today much to its original form as the Starbeck swimming baths. (S Abbott)

At the opening of The Prince of Wales Baths, Tomas Oxley, proprietor of the Knaresborough Spa Baths slashed his prices. This started a chain of events that led to campaigns by both parties to discredit each other. The Knaresborough Spa baths claimed purer water and Isaac Brunt of the Prince of Wales Baths reacted by claiming possession of the original spring. Both parties faced numerous lawsuits not to mention financial ruin. Then in the winter of 1879, in an attempt to outdo his rival by sinking another sulphur well, the owner of the Knaresborough Spa cut into a chalybeate spring and contaminated his main sulphur source for good. The Knaresborough spa fell into decline and was forced into complete closure in 1890. The Prince of Wales Baths continued to do business until 1939 by which time the general medical trend had left such establishments behind and Harrogate's spa industry was finished.

After the closure of the Knaresborough Spa the Harrogate Borough Council bought the property, along with the Prince of Wales Baths, and laid a pipeline from Starbeck to the Royal Baths to take the Starbeck waters to Low Harrogate. The buildings were then bought by Leonard Snowden who used them for his horse breeding and training business and later by a haulage contractor by the name of Fred Rushton who lived there until the early 1970s. This picture shows the buildings boarded up and awaiting demolition in the late 1970s. Fortunately decisive action was taken in the nick of time and the Department of the Environment awarded the buildings listed building status and the Knaresborough/ Starbeck Old spa was saved. (Starbeck Museum)

While carrying out demolition works to the Old Spa bathing block a heavy excavator caused an old underground tank to collapse resulting in a rather large and dangerous hole. (F Heaton)

The original chalybeate spring which is still there today and can be seen beside the wall by the Star Beck. (Starbeck Museum)

A closer look at the original sulphur spring that was marked with the pillar and basin during the mid 18th century. (S Abbott)

The remains of one of the Prince of Wales Baths sulphur springs. It is situated in the old park just behind the veterans' club hut. Everybody knows it is there but not many know what it is. (S Abbott)

The fully refurbished Starbeck Old spa buildings now the centre piece of the Spa mews old peoples complex. This quiet area of Starbeck retains a peaceful and historic atmosphere. To the right is the original 1823 bathhouse façade with the 1848 house to the left. (S Abbott)

The original 1823 archway that once welcomed hundreds of visitors daily to Starbeck's very own spa. (S Abbott)

Starbeck like any other working community has a fine tradition of good sport and recreation.

The all conquering Starbeck AFC of the 1903-04 season when they retained the Harrogate and District Football league championship with a record of played 29, won 26, drawn 1, lost 2. Such was their domination of local football during the early 1900s, that they were elected into the West Yorkshire league for the 1904-05 season, during which they played two matches against the newly formed Leeds City FC, the forerunner of Leeds United. One of the stars of this fine Starbeck side was Donald Simpson Bell (pictured 5th from the left) who went on to play for Mirfield, Bishop Auckland, Newcastle United and as a professional, Bradford Park Avenue while also serving as an assistant master at Starbeck School. For his services during the First World War, Donald Bell was awarded the Victoria Cross for actions described elsewhere in this book. Starbeck AFC who formed in 1900, originally played home games on a field with a steep slope off Forest Lane until moving to what was known as Lancaster Park in 1906, and eventually settling on the land now occupied by Shaw's trailer park. (Starbeck Museum)

Another pre First World War line up this time of Starbeck St Andrews FC. This church team became the premier Starbeck team in the Harrogate league after Starbeck AFC left to join the West Yorkshire League. (Starbeck Museum)

The Harrogate Golf Club moved from Irongate Bridge to Starbeck in 1898 opening their new course and club-house (middle) in 1899. The clubhouse was closed temporarily during 1905 due to an outbreak of smallpox and then extensively altered (bottom) during 1907 and 1908. Over the years many alterations have been made to both the clubhouse and the course transforming the Forest Lane Head club into a top quality golf club. (S Abbott postcard collection)

The laying out of the Starbeck pleasure grounds and municipal bowling green in the former spa grounds during 1907 led to the formation of the bowling club. The club is still running and competing in local competitions today and is as popular as ever. This picture taken during the 1920s shows a successful team with one of the many trophies won by the club over the years. (Starbeck Museum)

Starbeck is home to the Harrogate district's oldest public swimming baths. Here we see local born Jesse Colman, whose father managed the pool, pictured with the symbols of his success in 1918 the year he won the Harrogate Swimming Championship for the fourth consecutive time. (Starbeck Museum)

Another prominent local swimmer was Arthur Beaumont the British Plunging Champion who trained at Starbeck Baths. In later years he would become proprietor of Harrogate mineral water company, Barroclough's. (Starbeck Museum)

This picture was taken on the 18th July 1936 at the top of the High Street outside Starbeck School during the Harrogate 20 mile walking race. In the picture followed by a whole host of enthusiastic young cyclists is Hopkins of the Lancashire Walking Club who won the race and was subsequently picked for the 1936 Olympic games in Berlin. (W Smith/Starbeck Museum)

The Starbeck Council School Girls swimming team of the 1936 to 1937 season. Included here are Jessie Homes, Dorothy Morrell, Lois Brown, Agnes Charlesworth, Maureen Poole, Margaret Donegan, Betty Russell, Nita Brown, Thompson, Collier, Louise Baggueley, Eve Simpson and Joan Hawkes. (Starbeck Museum)

Starbeck Council School football team pictured around 1930. The young players are, Middle row: R Falkener, A Ferguson, Metcalf, D Sharpe, S Brecon, Outhwaite, Front row: D Earnshaw, R Andrews, Wilf Blakey, E Ibbotson, A Jordan. (W Blakey)

Starbeck Methodist United Football club, who in the years immediately before the Second World War had a remarkable run of success. Entering and winning the Harrogate and District League Division 5 in 1935 they went on to win the fourth, third, second and first divisions in consecutive years. (W Blakey)

The Starbeck Methodist United 1937 – 1938 season team. Back row L to R: Mr Pullan, Dawson, Abbott, Hawkes, Pybus, Dowson, G. Shutt, and W Johnson. Front row L to R: W Shutt, G Beer, J Blakey, W Blakey, A Dickinson (captain, with Harrogate & District League cup), Andrews, R Faulkner (W Blakey)

Starbeck Wednesday Football Club pictured in the mid 1930s. Back Row L to R: D Smerthwaite, D Midson, Henderson, V Boyce, Houseman, Front Row L to r: C Everitt, G Crowther, W Blakey, W Hudson, Clapham. (W Blakey)

Another 1930s' Starbeck team featuring the Blakey brothers was this Starbeck St. Andrews FC side. They played home matches on the St Andrews church athletic field that used to be opposite the end of Kingsley Road on land now occupied by the petrol station and Wedderburn Avenue. (W Blakey)

Pictured in the striped shirts are the Starbeck AFC. team of the 1925 – 26 season.
(Starbeck Museum)

Pictured here after winning a Harrogate and District cup final are the players and supporters of another 1930s' team Starbeck Council School Old Boys FC.
(Starbeck Museum)

The players of Starbeck LNER team, fore runners of the present Harrogate Railway Athletic FC, pictured here shortly after the formation of the club, waiting to board a Pyne's bus for a trip to Wembley. (Starbeck Museum)

Pictured outside the swimming baths between the wars are the Starbeck water polo team. Featured here are Mr Colman the baths manager and coach, his son Jesse who was Harrogate District Champion swimmer, British Plunging Champion Arthur Beaumont and the Sugden brothers Harry and Arthur. (Starbeck Museum)

The Starbeck Cycling Club was formed before the First World War and was still going strong throughout the inter war years when this picture featuring Albert Hodgson (seated) was taken. Albert Hodgson seen here being assisted by Fred Cann was a remarkable rider who would join the club on their regular rides to places as far away as Scarborough and Durham, despite having only one leg. (Starbeck Museum)

The Railway Cricket team of 1938. Back L to R: Fawcett, Addison, Anderson, Dickenson, Hardcastle, Leathley, Walker, Mann. Front L to R: Dobby, Powell, Kay, Wilkinson, Burgess.

Cricket had been played in Starbeck since the end of the 19th century. Originally the game was played in a field next to the railway lines on Forest Lane, then at what is now the School playing field and finally at the Railway grounds at Station View. Cricket died out in Starbeck during the mid 1970s and the old pavilion that was next to the Railway Athletic Clubhouse was pulled down shortly after. The Railway cricket team was formed around the same time as the football club in 1935. (Starbeck Museum)

The Railway Athletic team of 1948-49 with the trophies that prove their dominance of the local football scene during the days when they once won all 24 league games in a season. What is now known as Harrogate Railway Athletic Football Club was founded by a group of railway workers in 1935 as Starbeck LNER FC. They would soon become Starbeck's most influential sporting institution. Prior to 2002, the club's best season was the 1952-53 season when they won the Yorkshire League Cup and reached the dizzy heights of the Quarter Finals of the FA Amateur Cup beating Penrith and West Auckland along the way before defeat away at Harwich & Parkeston F C. (Starbeck Museum)

The Starbeck Working Men's Club darts team pictured in the 1950s with their season's silverware. Like any other working men's club the sport and games teams play a major role in the day to day running of the club. (SWMC)

The Railway Athletic team of 1956-57. Back Row L to R: D Hawkes, W Edwards, R Hill, G Thompson, G Sibson, J Elliott.   Front row L to R: W Everitt, A Everitt. J McEwan, P Reynard, K Fountain. The fifties were great times for "The Railway" who regularly took large numbers of supporters on "special" trains to away games. This team finished eleventh in the Yorkshire league division two but better consistency the next season led to a third place finish and promotion. Interestingly the 56-57 team were knocked out of the FA Cup for the third consecutive time by Goole Town each time away from home, each time in the second qualifying round. If you look into the background of this picture you will see the little stand, which stood between the pitch and the houses of Olive Grove, being erected. This stand, built to accommodate the enthusiastic crowds of the times, would last little over 10 years and would be pulled down around 1970. (Starbeck Museum)

The Railway Grounds at Station View have been used for many sporting events over the years: football, cricket, dog racing, athletics and even as this programme from August 1952 shows, Motorcycle racing. (Starbeck Museum)

The great Kip Keino of Kenya leads from England's Alan Simpson and Walter Wilkinson during the men's mile final at the 8th Commonwealth Games at Kingston Jamaica on the 13th August 1966. Walter Wilkinson was one of Britain's leading middle distance runners of the 1960s and early seventies. For a while during the sixties Wilkinson lived near the junction of Forest Lane and Forest Avenue. (Empics)

The one and only Beryl Burton, who was without a doubt the greatest women's cyclist of all time, pictured in October 1965 at the height of her fame. Between 1959 and 1983 Mrs Burton achieved an incredible 25 consecutive wins in the British all rounder competitions. She won the World Road Race Championship twice (in 1960 and 1967) and the World 3,000 metres Pursuit Championship five times (in 1959, 1960, 1962, 1963 and 1966). Having overcome serious illness Beryl Burton (who lived the later years of her life in Forest Lane Starbeck) died as the result of a cycling accident in Harrogate in May 1996 aged just 59. Shamefully Beryl Burton was never given (outside of her own sport) the recognition her achievements deserved and her death passed by with hardly a mention by the British media. (Empics)

In March 1997 a public cycleway that runs between the River Nidd and Bilton was opened and named in the honour of Beryl Burton, seven times World Cycling Champion. The route is popular among local cyclists and a constant reminder of her wonderful achievements. (S Abbott)

Railway's status slumped slightly during the 1970s dropping out of the Yorkshire league in 1973. The teams of the mid 1970s (above) had life in the Harrogate District leagues to contend with but things slowly started to improve and the teams of the 1980s (below) having gained re-entry to the Yorkshire League in 1980 became founder members of the Northern Counties East League in 1983 where they have remained ever since. (HRAFC)

Ironically the most picturesque corner of Starbeck is practically the only reminder of the railway industry that once filled Starbeck with so much activity. Situated off Bogs Lane in the triangle of the two lines is the old locomotive reservoir now known as the Kingsley Carp Waters where excellent fishing is enjoyed throughout the year.
(S Abbott)

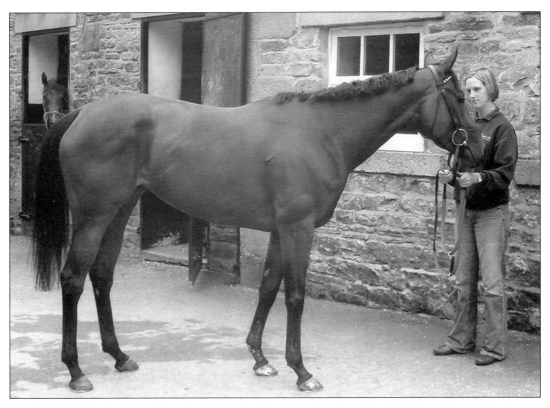

"Starbeck" ridden by David Harrison won the European Breeders Fund Maiden Stakes at York races in October 2000. Owned by Clarendon Racing and stabled at Middleham, North Yorkshire she was second at Newmarket in 2001 before suffering a lengthy absence from racing due to a serious leg injury. (Clarendon Racing)

The Nidd Valley Road Runners meet and run from the Railway Athletic club. Here we see the competitors of the 2000 annual Harrogate and District League race running along The Avenue shortly after the start and again along the old railway lines between Starbeck and Bilton. (www.Harrogate-league.co.uk)

The jubilant players of Harrogate Railway Athletic Football Club celebrate the greatest day in the 67 year history of the club on 28th October 2002, when they beat Marine FC of Merseyside by a fabulous 4-2 to qualify for the first round of the FA Cup for the first time in the club's history. Railway started the game as clear underdogs playing a team with a better pedigree from a higher league. On the day there was only one team in it and if anything 4-2 flattered Marine. (S Abbott)

Born on Wentworth Crescent, Mark Wilson went on to find success as an award winning groundsman, looking after the council sports facilities. Here he is with one of his awards after he won the West Riding and Northern Region groundsman of the year competitions for his work on the Killinghall Moor Football pitches. (Harrogate Advertiser)

At time of this book going to press, Railway Athletic had just won their first ever game in the FA Cup first round proper by defeating Slough Town away from home by two goals to one and were rewarded by receiving a home draw against Bristol City of the Football League division 2.

"FOR THE FUTURE PROSPERITY OF HIGH AND LOW HARROGATE, IT IS EXPEDIENT THAT NO RAILWAY SHOULD IN ANY CIRCUMSTANCES BE BROUGHT WITHIN THE IMMEDIATE PRECINCTS OF EITHER PLACE".

Such was the resolution unanimously passed at a special public meeting that took place at the Queen Hotel (now Cedar Court) in November 1844. The railways were coming, but not it seems to Harrogate. So it came to Starbeck instead, and Starbeck has never looked back.

Having opened partially a year previously, the Leeds to Thirsk railway opened fully in July 1849 with a station at Starbeck, and soon an engine shed, marshalling yards, goods, coal and livestock facilities sparked the rapid growth of our community as men from all round the country flocked here to work in some of the most important railway yards in the north of England.

The Station Master, his staff and the local policeman photographed on the down, (Harrogate bound) platform around the time of the start of the First World War. This side of the railway station was built of red brick and dates from 1848 when the Leeds to Thirsk line was opened between Ripon and Weeton. The station was fully manned with porters, and ticket office staff etc, and included waiting rooms, conveniences and even Starbeck's first post office. With the introduction of conductor/guards all staff were withdrawn from Starbeck station on 15 June 1969. (Starbeck Museum)

A railway worker and a passenger await an oncoming train on the up (Knaresborough bound) platform around 1920. The buildings on this side were of a wooden construction and were built when the station was extended and the canopy erected in 1898. (S Abbott postcard collection)

A 1950s shot of the railway station taken from the end of Spa Lane, showing the old signal gantry, the wooden gates and the station master's house. Following a fatal accident where a young woman was killed crossing the lines in 1882 a footbridge was erected on the site of the gantry. The bridge was replaced by the subway in 1903. (Starbeck Museum)

This bridge was built in 1848 and crossed Hookstone Chase at the exact spot of the Morrisons roundabout. The Starbeck to Pannal section of the old Leeds & Thirsk railway closed when the Low Crimple Viaduct was found to be unsafe in 1951. The bridge remained in place until demolition around 1970. (Starbeck Museum)

Locomotive number 166 pictured in Starbeck north yard while on service here between 1920 and 1950 when it was transferred to Stockton, before being withdrawn from service in 1958. Where the engine stands is now part of the Station View old peoples complex and the houses just visible in the background are The Avenue. (G Pierson collection)

Two elderly residents take advantage of a lull in the traffic to cross the road by the Trans-shipment shed in 1973. Trains would come into these sheds fully loaded with goods in bulk to be split up here into smaller lots to be despatched on separate trains to their final destinations. (Moyra Osborne)

Engine no 67337 pulling passenger coaches awaits the signal to pull off for York. (Ken Hoole collection/NERA)

Starbeck south signal box pictured around 1962. The signal box was severely damaged in 1893 when a Darlington bound goods train ran through the buffers and crashed, coming to a halt nine feet inside the signal box completely wrecking the signal mechanism. The signalman escaped injury by jumping out of the opposite window.

Miraculously nobody was injured when a runaway train from the Harrogate yard crashed through the crossing gates during the rush hour on the 3rd March 1972. The present barriers replaced wooden gates in 1974 (Ken Hoole collection/NERA)

Surrounded by locomotives, the Starbeck loco shed pictured in its original form sometime in the 1920s. This stood in the south yard between Prospect Road and Spa Road. The Starbeck shed opened soon after the arrival of the railways and closed with the rest of the south yard on 13th September 1959. (Ken Hoole collection/NERA)

The Starbeck loco shed seen here after refurbishment in the late 1950s. The walls were raised and a new roof was provided but the shed closed for good in 1959. Soon after closure the roof was removed and re-erected at Holbeck Leeds. This left the walls unstable and the west wall blew down in the gales of 1962 and the remainder of the building was demolished soon after. (Ken Hoole collection/NERA)

The famous 60023 A4 "Golden Eagle" with a full train of passenger coaches passes through Starbeck station on a diverted journey during the golden years of steam. The old Leeds and Thirsk line was well connected to the main line stations of York, Leeds, and the North East and mainline passenger trains were often diverted this way in times of crisis. (J W Armstrong trust)

This April 1949 picture shows the view from the end of the Starbeck up platform looking towards Bilton. The Starbeck north signal box can be seen, which marked the junction of the Harrogate and Ripon lines. A small section of the lines into the north yard can also be seen (J W Armstrong Trust)

The Starbeck station photographed looking towards the High Street. The 1962 view (above) shows some of the original 1848 brick built station buildings behind the down platform and at the very right of the shot the corner of the trans-shipment shed. Dating from 1972 a closer look at the down platform (below) clearly shows the 1898 wooden construction of the buildings and the entrances to the waiting, porters' and guards' rooms. (Ken Hoole collection/NERA)

This 1972 shot of the up platform from the level crossing shows much of the original 1848 station building. Also visible is evidence of the original platform level. The platform was raised when the station was extended and the canopy erected in 1898. The lower (original) level of the platform was of a stone construction with the extension clearly visible in red brick. The raising of the platform left the station buildings at a lower level and older readers may remember the step down into the station rooms. (Ken Hoole collection/NERA)

This sad scene was photographed during the winter of 1978-1979 when the old station, already minus the canopy, was in the early stages of demolition. The station had been unmanned since 1969, and had fallen into disrepair due to natural deterioration and vandalism. (J W Armstrong trust)

As several local residents have reported, on visits to the railway museum at Oxenhope an original Starbeck luggage trolley can be seen.   (Starbeck Museum)

Richard Clifford and his trusty workmate "Trigger" await yet another load of coal at the loading dock in the old coal yard adjoining the goods depot. (Moyra Osborne)

During the mid 1980s The Railway Preservation Society was given access by Octavius Atkinson & Sons to part of the old Starbeck south yard. Here they restored engines, carriages and rolling stock. They also re-laid lengths of track and excavated around the old turntable and loco shed. During their regular open days they would give rides on one of their reconditioned engines. Sadly when Octavius Atkinson's moved out of Starbeck the land was sold and the Railway Preservation Society had to move on. The area is now taken up by Sycamore Drive and the children's play area at the bottom end of First Avenue. (Starbeck Museum)

Today's bleak and featureless station. The bare and open platforms with their 1980s bus shelter like facilities are less than a shadow of the station's former grandeur. (S Abbott)

To mark the extent of our community and reminding us of days gone by Starbeck boundary markers were laid in the summer of 1998. The markers were made around a replica locomotive wheel and bear a heraldic coat of arms design depicting a star, water and a locomotive. Starbeck had never before had boundary markers and these at Crossways (pictured), Forest Lane Head, and the junction of Knaresborough Road and Kingsley Road serve to mark Starbeck as the separate community, quite apart from the rest of Harrogate, that it has always been. (S Abbott)

Community Celebrations

In years gone by Starbeck like any other community has held parades for many reasons. In celebration, in anger, in remembrance or just for the fun of it, a parade always catches the attention of the people.

It is true that due to the loss of participating local companies, in recent times our annual gala parade has decreased in numbers year after year. Yet the event itself still flourishes and remains the most popular community event of the year.

As the spectators overcrowd the wide high street footpaths and spill onto the road, a parade stands in readiness during the St Andrews festival of 1906. At the front with the banner are representatives of the St Andrews Church Sunday School. Next in line is the Starbeck Brass Band.

The four shops nearest the camera are Charles Jackson's Dairy, Wilby and Co the Tailors, J Hannam Plumber and Glazier, and Lockwood Brothers Second Hand Furniture Dealership. These four stood together from 1905 to 1907 and firmly date the picture as 1906. (Starbeck Museum)

Another early parade this time pictured just approaching the railway station from the direction of Harrogate. Leading the parade is the Starbeck Brass Band followed by what appears to be the local Brownies and Girl Guides followed by the Boy Scouts. A group of children march along with the band and in the rear the St Andrews Sunday School banner can just be seen. The Starbeck Brass Band were formed by Samuel Day in 1904 and after rehearsing in a house on Stonefall Avenue found a more permanent home on Back Regent Place in 1906. (Starbeck Museum)

During the early summer of 1935 celebrations were held to mark the silver jubilee of King George V. Pictured here outside the Working Men's Club on Forest Avenue are the members' children who took part in a fancy dress parade. The four children to the front are Louie, Denis, Jim, and Merle Coleman. Jim Coleman (dressed as a Red Indian) is now club secretary. (Harrogate Advertiser)

May 10th 1937. To mark the coronation of King George VI all the schools in the Harrogate area formed a procession, each float representing a country of the British Empire. Starbeck's contribution represented Wales. The children include Robert Hornby, William Bookless, Arthur Wilde (standing) Betty Chatten, Mabel Symonds and Jean Ingrey. (Starbeck Museum)

During the 1960s and 70s the gala was held on the Railway Athletic field. Here we see the 1973 float from the Harrogate Hotel, which in everyday use was Richard Clifford's coal wagon. Also from 1973 two well known local lady participants. (Moyra Osborne)

The Prince of Wales public house tug of war team that took on all comers at the annual bank holiday gala of 1995, which included Andy Wetherall, Carl Hawksby, Dick Dalby, Alex Baronovski and Andy Woodall, are pictured on the gala field with landlady Peggy Winters.   (Prince of Wales)

This picture was taken in the late 1990s at the opening of the newly refurbished children's play area on Belmont Field. Pictured here are campaigning children and parents along with councillors Barry Haxby, Reg Marsh, Pat Marsh, and Phillip Broadbank with Mrs Broadbank. To allay claims that local politicians are old fashioned, I must clarify that our councillors were dressed to take part in the Starbeck Edwardian day celebrations that were held on the same day. (P Marsh)

The theme of the 1997 gala was sport. The Mayor of Harrogate presented first prize in the best float competition to the "Art of Hair" salon entry for their attempts at human snooker. From the start at Camwal Road the parade crosses the High Street and follows Forest Avenue and Forest Lane to Forest Lane Head then back down Knaresborough Road to Belmont Field where the gala has been held since the early 1980s. (S Abbott)

The Gala Queen of 2000 Emma Swales pictured here with her attendants Amy Collins and Jenny Price. (C Abbott)

The year 2002. The Gala Queen was 13-year-old Jessica Whitehead and the two nine-year-old attendants were Sarah Linfoot and Abbey Whitehead. (S Abbott)

The theme of 2002 was the Queen's golden jubilee. The Starbeck Conservative Club, who received their prize from the Mayor of Harrogate, Councillor Alan Skidmore, won the best float competition. (Harrogate Advertiser)

The St Andrews Church float and their all singing and dancing entourage was for many one of the highlights of the 2002 parade (right and opposite top). (S Abbott)

Raising large amounts of money for local charities the Gala event is always well attended and generally blessed with sunshine. Along with children's rides, bouncy castles and face painting there are always the more traditional stalls and games of skill and chance. Races for the children and football competitions along with pet shows and line dancing displays entertain the crowds. (S Abbott)

Local lads Dave Collins (left) and Brian Owen posing at their coconut shy. The money raised by this and the other stalls benefits local charities and also goes towards the Bonfire Night firework display and the Christmas lights.

Without them there would be no Gala. To the right in the Union jack shirt is Granville Ward, event organiser and Starbeck councillor. At the back is the Silver Dollar line-dancing troupe who along with the majorettes and the White Rose Squares entertained the crowds in the arena. At front left we have the gala queen and attendants with the Mayor of Harrogate, Councillor Alan Skidmore behind. Also here are some of the many participants of the parade and fancy dress. (Harrogate Advertiser)

Another major public event in 2002 was the Queen's golden jubilee. Here the children of Starbeck Primary School gather for their special party lunch in the playground with their tables and chairs set out in the shape of the Union flag. (Harrogate Advertiser)

Meanwhile at Hookstone Chase Primary School the pupils dressed up for their special jubilee lunch. Dressed all in red, white and blue they pose here in front of their drawings and poems of the Queen. (Harrogate Advertiser)

At first things looked bleak for the residents of the Wentworth Estate who were pictured here when things looked their worst. Their year long plans for a jubilee street party seemed scuppered when after having their jubilee funding application turned down due to a mountain of red tape, they were further disappointed when they found out the gas board planned to dig up the street. However all turned out well and the party went ahead with a fine feast, fun and games on the playing field, and a good old party in the church hall. (Harrogate Advertiser)

The 20th century was a century of destruction as far as Starbeck's larger, more substantial houses were concerned. Belmont House, Belmont Villa, Forest Grange, The Grove, Harrison Hill House, Stonefall Manor, all fell victim of the wrecking ball. Though the majority of the Victorian terrace houses still remain the 1950s and 60s saw the demise of Old Beck Street and Camwal Road. What is left is something of a mixed bag, some large houses, some small, some old houses and some new.

Photographed around the beginning of the First World War we see here The Avenue viewed from Knaresborough Road. Built during the 1880s this end of the Avenue was originally known as Albert Avenue, with the far end being Victoria Avenue. The two joined together and the name was shortened in 1904 at the same time as Bower Road, Beech Grove and Albert Terrace were re-named to avoid confusion after Starbeck became part of the Borough of Harrogate in 1900. (S Abbott postcard collection)

A Christmas card of the early 1920s depicting the High Street from the railway crossing looking towards High Harrogate. To the right of the shot are the earliest of the railway goods buildings while just left of centre in the background we can see the old chimney of Atkinson's 19th-century steam corn mill (now the video rental store), though at the time of this picture the mill had closed and formed the Harrogate Pure Ice Company's ice factory where they used steam to power the production of ice using ammonia. (S Abbott postcard collection)

A 1922 view of the upper High Street this time looking toward the Ice factory (right) from the St Andrews church field (now Wedderburn Avenue) The houses to the left were all built between 1900 and 1910. The row of fine beech trees gave the area the original name of Beech Grove. The trees were all cut down during the late 1950s after one fell down during a storm rendering the rest dangerous.

This 1910 view of Albert Place interestingly shows the pole of Lister's barbershop at number 3 and William Appleton's building, joinery and undertaking business at number 5. Outside the barber shop and halfway down the street we see the original, gas lights while at the extreme right we can just make out the boundary wall and part of the old Primitive Methodist Church. (S Abbott postcard collection)

Two 1920s views of Stonefall Avenue looking both East (above) and West (below). The scene today is unchanged with the exception of the old gaslights. When first built during the late 19th century the first block of houses on the Harrogate side was known as Beechwood Terrace and the houses opposite, to the Starbeck side were known as Stonefall Terrace. The remainder of the road was Stonefall Avenue, and the whole lot were renumbered as Stonefall Avenue in 1904 (S Abbott postcard collection)

The summer of 1973 and a fully loaded coal wagon stands on the weighbridge of Clifford's Coal Yard. There had been a coal yard here since the coming of the railways in 1849 and Richard Clifford ran his business here from 1958 until the yard closed and was eventually demolished with the rest of the railway goods facilities and the station in 1978. (Moyra Osborne)

Avenue Road in the mid 1970s. These houses were built over a 20 year period between 1882 and 1902 to house the large number of people coming into the area to work on the booming railways. In the background some of the slaughterhouse buildings can still be seen. (Jim Rogers)

Two mid 1970s views of the back street between Grove Street and Globe Street. E A Greenwood's butchers van, ready for loading, waits at the back of the old slaughterhouse. The abattoir closed down in the early 1990s due to new European regulations and the empty building was quickly demolished to make way for modern housing. (Jim Rogers)

This Art Deco style building on the upper High Street started life in the 1920s as the Electric Company show rooms, but has served as a second hand car dealership for many years. (S Abbott)

Getting Together

H ere we have a look at just a few of the hundreds of groups and associations that have gathered throughout the 20th century for so many reasons. Some gather for charitable reasons, some for other worthwhile causes while some are just for the fun of it and the enjoyment of each other's company.

The building in the background of this 1920s photograph is long gone now. This is the choir of the Primitive Methodist church outside their Church building, which stood on the corner of Albert Place and the High Street in the space today occupied by the row of 1960s' shops with flats above. (Starbeck Museum)

Proudly displaying what is most likely some form of award, the ladies of the St. Andrews Church Mothers Union Choir. This picture was taken in the years leading up to World War Two and is especially interesting because it contains a view of the old Primitive Methodist Church in the background and the present St Andrews Church to the left of the group which includes Mrs Iddison, Mrs Binks, Mrs Sugden, Mrs Traves, Mrs Curry, Mrs Outhwaite, Mrs Smurthwaite, Mrs Lancaster and Mrs Watson though nine ladies remain unknown. (Starbeck Museum)

Another Mothers Union get together sometime during the 1950s/60s. The venue of this picture, possibly an outing is unknown other than it certainly isn't in Starbeck. The ladies include; the Mrs' Bailes, Winterburn, Sugden, Lawson, Pratt, Brown, Ferguson, Greenwood, Briggs, Gammons, Wallis, Goodyear, Watson, Rowe, Dinnis, Sleight, Dean, Overton, Watson, Hawkes, Nightingale and Fisher. Again a number of ladies remain unnamed, as do the two gentlemen who would possibly prefer the anonymity. (Starbeck Museum)

Not a social group but an Octavius Atkinson and Sons staff photograph taken shortly after the outbreak of World War Two. Mr Atkinson, son of the original Octavius, sits front centre flanked by his sons. As you can see many women came into the structural steelwork factory during the war years when production switched over to war work. As their contribution to the war effort they produced a portable harbour, an aircraft landing strip, a number of floating "Bailey" bridges and tank landing craft, all used during the Normandy landings of 1944. Many of the women stayed on after the war, one or two until retirement. The company that began in a blacksmith's shop near Masham in the 19th century before moving to Tower Street and Robert Street and to Prospect road in 1938, relocated to Flaxby Moor in 1990 before closing completely in 1993. (Starbeck Museum)

The St Andrews Church schoolrooms have for so many years been home for the 5th Harrogate Cubs and Scouts. This 1930s picture shows the local troop gathering outside their meeting hall on Belmont Avenue, the official name of what we know today as the church car park. The trees behind border Addyman's field and beyond them can be seen the brick houses of The Avenue and the houses of 77-81 High Street still with their distinctive white tile work decoration now almost completely rendered and painted out. (Starbeck Museum)

A group of young friends play on the swings that used to be on the school playing field until the outbreak of World War two. The five young boys are unknown but the man standing on the left is school caretaker Walter Smith. (Starbeck Museum)

The local Cubs pose around their barrow during the Second World War. The picture shows them on the back streets behind Regent Place collecting scrap metal for the war effort. (Starbeck Museum)

The 1964 Scout Gangshow at the St Andrews church schoolroom. There were other scout troops present but the Starbeck (5th Harrogate) troop can be recognised by their dark (blue) neckerchiefs that were crossed once with a white lanyard to signify the cross of St Andrew. The man in the bow tie at the centre of the second row is the gangshow producer E L Kennedy-Bruyneels who lived at Harlow Park. Sat to the left of Mr Bruyneels is assistant scout master John Brazier and two to the right of the producer is scoutmaster Len Heaton who also ran the Starbeck Boy's Club on The Avenue. (Starbeck Museum)

As an alternative to the Boy Scouts, and meeting in the Methodist Church, the Boy's Brigade has also played its part in the development of our young men. This 1962 picture shows them with leader Ernie McGrellis picking up yet another award. The Boys Brigade band was always a feature at local parades. (Starbeck Museum)

For many members of the Scouts and Boy's Brigade, the highlight of the year is the annual camps. Here we see the members of the Boys Brigade at camp in 1962 (above) and 1968 (below). (Starbeck Museum)

After the Methodist union of 1931, the Salvation Army used part of the old Primitive Methodist Church for meetings. This 1930s picture shows the ladies choir outside the meeting hall. (Starbeck Museum)

The Salvation Army Junior band of the 1930s pictured here after practice outside the meeting hall on Albert Place. (Starbeck Museum)

Amateur dramatics has always had a place in Starbeck society. This picture shows the finale of "The Pirates of Penzance" in the school hall, performed by the Starbeck Operatic Society in January 1930. Since 1969 the St Andrews players have rehearsed in the St Andrews school rooms and performed annual musical productions at various venues including the St Andrews hall, Granby School, the Royal Hall and Harrogate Theatre. (S Abbott postcard collection)

For many generations of Starbeck children one of the highlights of the year has always been the Starbeck Mission Sunday School trip, and going by the number of W Pyne's coaches this 1950s' outing must have been a very well attended trip. W Pyne's White Coach tours started in the early 1900s on Camwal Road Starbeck and soon became the district's premier coach company. The company was sold to Wray's coaches in the 1980s. (Starbeck Museum)

The Starbeck Working Men's Club, who celebrated its centenary in 2001, has occupied the same position at number 4 Forest Avenue ever since formation in 1901. Originally the premises were leased but after just 10 years the committee voted to take up an opportunity to buy the building in 1911. Throughout the following decades the club has expanded and grown. This picture shows the full committee of 1975.

Back Row L to R: G Beadle, J Grayson, J Wray, F Lunn, D Wainwright, R Clarke, B Steel, J Moore, and K Wilson

Front Row L to R: B Sadler, A Smith, C Sample, J H Homes (secretary) R Cooper (president) T Bland, H Pedel, W Sadler. (SWMC)

Sports and games are always a big part of life for the members of any Working Men's Club, with snooker, billiards, pool, darts, dominoes, and even a fishing section on offer there is always plenty of competition between the membership and as representative teams against other pubs and clubs. This picture from the 1970s shows the Christmas Handicap winners with their trophies. (SWMC)

Throughout the years, the many club trips have always been well attended. The annual trip for members and families to the seaside has, on occasions, left Starbeck like a ghost town, and there are many smaller group trips throughout the year. This picture shows an enthusiastic group of sporting members on a 1980 visit to Headingley for the Leeds v Hull rugby league game. (SWMC)

Starbeck is also home to a number of fine and still traditional public houses, the regular customers of which are only too willing to join in the sports, games and other festivities that take place throughout the year. This picture shows landlady Peggy Winters with the Prince of Wales' tug of war team. Included in the picture taken at the annual gala are local strong men. Back Row L to R: Mick Lawson, Chris Swales, Leighton Hindes, Ian Shaw, Nick Parker, Jason Callingham, Mark ????.
  Front Row L to R: Tony Broadbent and Andy Dean. (Prince of Wales)

Saturday March 11th 1978. As the concluding act to a campaign organised by Andrew Stalker, children and parents gathered to demonstrate their disapproval towards a controversial proposal by the Harrogate Borough Council to redevelop the "Cat's Field" on Forest Lane. The plan was to use this playing field for the site of the construction of a residential home for the elderly. The success of the campaign resulted in the adoption of an alternative scheme, which led to the demolition of the redundant railway sheds and the development of the Station View complex. The Cat's Field has a history of its own. Allotment gardens here were closed in 1967 as part of a scheme to provide a (still) much-needed bypass for the level crossing on the High Street. The bypass was never built and the former allotments soon became derelict. This land soon attracted a great number of stray cats, hence the name. The derelict allotments were transformed into a children's football pitch around 1970. (Starbeck Museum)

Gorden Beer & The Starbeck Museum

Writing books about Starbeck and working in the museum brings it home to me that I have a tough act to follow. Everyone I meet gives me an impression of the deep affection the community holds for Gordon Beer. There have been many men and women in the past who have served Starbeck well, James Chippindale, John Houfe, James Addyman and a whole list of characters and personalities right up to the present day, but there will always be a special place in the hearts of the people who knew Gordon Beer for the man so fondly dubbed "Mr Starbeck".

Gordon Beer, a lifelong member of the Methodist church, was in his youth a Sunday school teacher and chapel organist. He first became known to the Harrogate public in 1947 when he returned to the town after his time in the armed forces to take a teaching post at New Park School. He quickly rose to the position of head of the Maths and PE departments. At the opening of Granby Park Secondary Modern School in 1965 he was appointed Senior Master and Head of Maths. Then at the amalgamation of Granby Park and the High School to form Granby High Comprehensive School he was appointed Head of the middle school.

A Starbeck resident since 1955 he wrote his first book, a history of the Starbeck Methodist Church in 1981. Retiring from teaching in 1982 a year later he wrote the book 'The Village of Starbeck' in 1983. Another three books and over a 150 talks and lectures would follow as Mr Beer busied himself with local history and soon found himself in the position where he could never walk more than a couple of yards down Starbeck High Street before somebody stopped him to talk over the old days. This was something he enjoyed and he always had time for anybody he met.

Soon the artefacts and pictures that people were giving him led him, working along side Starbeck School Headmaster Desmond Hardcastle, to initiate the Starbeck Museum. This was housed in the building to the right of the main school entrance that was originally built as the headmaster's lodgings.

The museum opened on the 7th June 1996 and has been a popular local amenity ever since. In the meantime Gordon Beer was also the driving force behind the campaign that led to the refurbishment of the war memorial and the revival of the Armistice Day parade.

Sadly Mr Beer passed away in 1999 leaving behind a legacy that is difficult to follow.

A picture taken June 7th 1996 shows Gordon Beer at the opening of the Museum. Always ready to help the young, Mr Beer gives Chris Ternant the benefit of his knowledge. (Harrogate Advertiser)

The crowds gather on a sunny Saturday in Prospect Park, May 11th 2002 to witness the unveiling of the Gordon Beer memorial.   (S Abbott)

Mrs Daphne Beer and Harrogate Member of Parliament Phil Willis prepare to cut a specially prepared cake at the unveiling of the Gordon Beer memorial. (S Abbott)

The Gordon Beer Memorial in Prospect Park. Unveiled on May 11th 2002 before a crowd of admirers wishing to take the opportunity to pay their respects, the idea of the memorial was instigated and carried out by the Starbeck in Bloom committee and paid for by donations from a grateful public. (S Abbott)

The Starbeck Museum building was built in 1895 with the rest of the school and was initially the headmaster's house. Many more recent ex-pupils will remember the building being used by the school nurse for her duties and many had cookery or music lessons there. The Museum first opened on June 7th 1996 and still opens on Wednesday evenings during the school summer holidays. The museum is also available to organised groups who will find an informative and dedicated team ready to help with any enquiries. (S Abbott)

Views of the inside of the museum. (S Abbott)

Starbeck In Bloom

Having recently won the Yorkshire in Bloom Urban Community section for the second time the Starbeck in Bloom team are proving to be something of a local success story.

To celebrate their 2002 triumph the Starbeck in Bloom committee and local council officials gather around another of their fine works, the Gordon Beer memorial in Prospect Park. From the left are Chairman Elliott Clark, Harrogate District Parks Supervisor John Shepherd, Community Liaison Officer Sue Wood, Marjorie Hutton, Christine Stewart, Margaret Algie from Springwater School (who won the Sir Richard Graham Youth Enterprise award for their woodland walk), Harrogate District Parks Area Manager Andrew Soper, and Chris Binks. (Harrogate Advertiser)

Another example of their good work is the annual Starbeck in Bloom Flower, Fruit and Vegetable Show. Winner of the 2002 best onions in show section, Mike Walmsley receives the Ron Robson memorial cup from Shirley Snape and Chairman Elliott Clark. (Harrogate Advertiser)

Eric Tillet (now there's a name for a gardener), with his prize-winning leeks. Mr Tillet won both first and second prizes for his leeks in the August 2002 show, and then went on to win the best allotment competition a month later. (Harrogate Advertiser)

Starbeck in Bloom secretary Christine Stewart (left) presents the Irene Winstanley trophy to Jean Tillet, whose delicious coconut cake claimed first prize at the 2002 show. (Harrogate Advertiser)

Pictured here are Sally Davis, Margaret Roberts, and Jane Taylor from the day centre at Station view who won first prize in September 2002 in the Starbeck in Bloom containers, baskets and flowerbed section. The annual competition has many categories that include best front gardens, both large and small, best back garden, best allotment, and best community and business garden.
(Harrogate Advertiser)

The Bells Are Ringing

Regardless of our beliefs all our lives are affected by religion, and Starbeck like anywhere else has a strong, varied, and rich religious history.

Under the direction of the remarkable Miss Charlotte Harrison this building opened as a Sunday school in 1857 and soon after became Starbeck's earliest Anglican chapel. Situated on Forest Lane, this chapel, (now numbers 75 and 77 Forest Lane) served the community for more than thirty years until overcrowding led to the building of a new church on the present St Andrews site in 1888/89. The old chapel remained in public service for many years both as a school, and a Sunday school. (St Andrews)

Consecrated on St Andrew's day 1889 and serving as a chapel of ease attached to Christ Church the first St Andrews church was itself becoming overcrowded by the early 1900s. By 1905 plans were afoot to establish Starbeck as a separate parish and replace this church with a larger building. This building was demolished to make way for the present church in 1909. (St Andrews)

Laying the foundation stone of the present church after demolition of the earlier church in 1909. The new church was consecrated in August 1910, and Starbeck received separate parish status in December 1911. (St Andrews)

The Primitive Methodist church at Starbeck opened at the corner of Albert Place and the High Street in 1879. The main part of the building was demolished shortly after union with the Wesleyan Methodists in 1931. A small section was spared and was home to the local Salvation Army corps. until the early 1960s when the remainder of the building was removed to make way for the present shops and flats.

This building, now the public library, began life in April 1889 as the Wesleyan Methodist church. It was built with a small schoolroom to the rear, at a combined cost of £800. Previously Wesleyan services had been held at Forest Lane Head. Monthly local temperance meetings were also held in the Avenue Church. The two halves of the Methodist church were united in Starbeck in 1931 when this church became redundant, and the newly united Methodists moved into the present church on the High Street. (S Abbott)

Joseph Johnson presides over a harvest festival in the Wesleyan Methodist church on The Avenue during the early years of the 20th century. (Starbeck Museum)

The present Methodist church which officially opened on 24th June 1931 to house the recently united Primitive and Wesleyan Methodists. (S Abbott)

Revd K I Ford, the popular minister of Starbeck
Methodist church from 1952 to 1958.
(Starbeck Museum)

The Mayoress receives a bouquet from a young pupil at the opening of the new Railway (now Starbeck)
Mission Sunday school extension in August 1932. The Railway Mission began life in a station waiting
room in the 1880s before moving to a converted stable on Spa Lane until the Forest Avenue mission
room was completed in 1910. After serving the religious needs of railway workers and their families
for many years the Railway Mission reacted to the closure of the railway facilities during the 1950s by
renaming to Starbeck Mission in 1960. (Harrogate Advertiser)

Children of the Railway mission Sunday school of 1936.

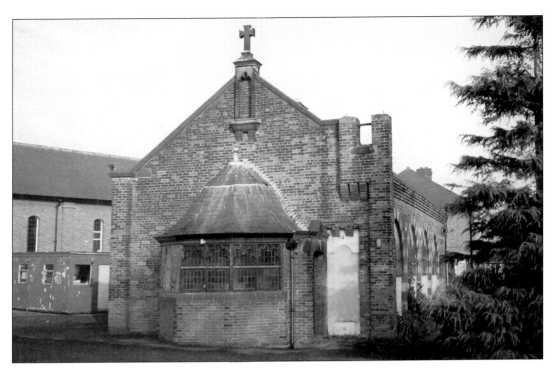

The first Catholic Church, dedicated to St Aeldred of Rievaulx (above) was built at the juncture of Stonefall Avenue and Wedderburn Drive and opened in 1912. The original building, now used as a parish hall was succeeded by the present church and presbytery (below), designed by Ronchetti, in 1957. (S Abbott)

An elderly couple of the day takes time out from exercising their dog to pose in this late 1900s photograph taken just inside the recently opened Starbeck Pleasure grounds. These gardens situated on Spa Lane opened to the public in June 1907 having been created from the former Prince of Wales Baths gardens. (S Abbott post card collection)

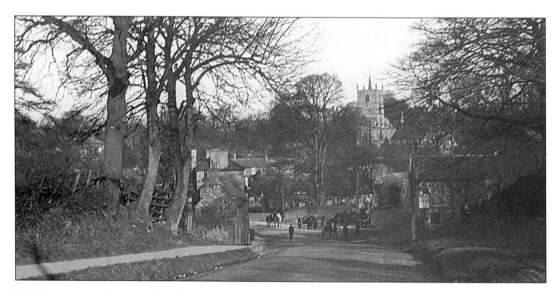

This interesting photograph, taken some time during the 1930s shows the Road from Starbeck as it enters Knaresborough. Clearly visible before the George Hotel (now Yorkshire lass) public house is a small row of former Almshouses now sadly long since demolished. (S Abbott post card collection)

Dated 1905. These two pictures were taken from the same place at the very bottom of the High Street, (above) looking towards Knaresborough and showing all the shops along with the recently rebuilt Star Inn. While the other (below) shows the road leading to High Harrogate. Clearly visible are the original railway buildings and the chimney from Atkinson's steam corn mill that was by then converted to the production of ice for business and household use. (S Abbott postcard collection)

After being acquired by the Harrogate Borough Council in 1900 to allow them to pump the waters to the Royal baths, the former Starbeck (Karesborough) Old spa building was sold into private ownership. From 1901 to 1936 it was the home and business premises of Leonard Snowden (Horse Dealer) who converted the old 1823 bathhouses into stables.

There had never been a team from Harrogate in the first round proper of the F A Cup until the 2002-2003 season, when our very own Harrogate Railway Athletic F C reached the unprecedented heights of the second round. The run came to an end on Sunday 8th December 2002 when the gallant team finally succumbed to a 3-1 home defeat by Bristol City of the Football League 2nd Division. The great adventure ended not with sadness but a great sense of achievement as the "live" Sky television cameras showed a brave fight back from 2-0 down to 2-1 courtesy of a Steve Davey goal. As railway fought tooth and nail for an equaliser Bristol broke forward and in the dying minutes made the score a flattering 3-1 in their favour. The team ended the afternoon by taking a lap of honour to the rapturous applause of the 3500 home fans who appreciated the achievement of our little team who had won six games to get so far (the same number of games Arsenal played that season to win the trophy). (HRAFC)

Index

LANDM▲RK
COLLECTOR'S LIBRARY

LANDM▲RK
Publishing Ltd ● ● ● ●

Ashbourne Hall, Cokayne Ave, Ashbourne, Derbyshire, DE6 1EJ England□
Tel 01335 347349 Fax 01335 347303 □
e-mail landmark@clara.net web site: www.landmarkpublishing.co.uk

Mining Histories

- Cheadle Coalfield, Staffordshire, The History of the   *ISBN: 1 84306 013 2, £19.95*
- Churnet Valley Iron, The mills & the mines   *ISBN: 1 84306 011 6, paperback, £9.95*
- Collieries of South Wales: Vol 1   *ISBN: 1 84306 015 9, £22.50*
- Collieries of South Wales: Vol 2   *ISBN: 1 84306 017 5, £19.95*
- Collieries of Somerset & Bristol   *ISBN: 1 84306 029 9, £14.95*
- Copper & Lead Mines around the Manifold Valley, North Staffordshire   *ISBN: 1 901522 77 6, £19.95*
- Images of Cornish Tin   *ISBN: 1 84306 020 5, £29.95*
- Lathkill Dale, Derbyshire, its Mines and Miners   *ISBN: 1 901522 80 6, £8.00*
- Rocks & Scenery the Peak District   *ISBN: 1 84306 026 4, paperback, £7.95*
- Victorian Slate Mining   *ISBN: 1 84306 073 6, £15.95*

Industrial Histories

- Richard Roberts, The Life & Inventions of, 1789 - 1864   *ISBN: 1 84306 027 2, £29.95*
- The Textile Mill Engine   *ISBN: 1 901522 43 1, paperback, £22.50*
- Watt, James, His Life in Scotland, 1736-74   *ISBN 1 84306 045 0, £35.00*
- Wolseley, The Real, Adderley Park Works, 1901-1926   *ISBN 1 84306 052 3, £19.95*

Roads & Transportantion

- Packmen, Carriers & Packhorse Roads   *ISBN: 1 84306 016 7, £19.95*
- Roads & Trackways of Wales   *ISBN: 1 84306 019 1, £22.50*
- Welsh Cattle Drovers   *ISBN: 1 84306 021 3, £22.50*
- Peakland Roads & Trackways   *ISBN: 1 901522 91 1, £19.95*

Regional/Local Histories

- Derbyshire Country Houses: Vol 1   *ISBN: 1 84306 007 8, £19.95*
- Derbyshire Country Houses: Vol 2   *ISBN: 1 84306 041 8, £19.95*
- Lost Houses of Derbyshire   *ISBN: 1 84306 064 7, £19.95*
- Well Dressing   *ISBN: 1 84306 042 6, Full colour, £19.95*
- Crosses of the Peak District   *ISBN 1 84306 044 2, £14.95*
- Shrovetide Football and the Ashbourne Game   *ISBN: 1 84306 063 9, £19.95*
- Historic Hallamshire   *ISBN: 1 84306 049 3, £19.95*
- Colwyn Bay, Its History across the Years   *ISBN: 1 84306 014 0, £24.95*
- Llandudno: Queen of Welsh Resorts   *ISBN 1 84306 048 5, £15.95*
- Llanrwst: the History of a Market Town   *ISBN 1 84306 070 1, £14.95*
- Lost Houses in and around Wrexham   *ISBN 1 84306 057 4, £16.95*
- Shipwrecks of North Wales   *ISBN: 1 84306 005 1, £19.95*